Answers to Potters' Questions

Answers to Potters' Questions

Selected from the Ceramics Monthly Questions Column

Edited by
Barbara Tipton

© Copyright 1990
Professional Publications, Inc.
1609 Northwest Boulevard, Columbus, Ohio 43212

Publishers of CERAMICS MONTHLY

PRINTED IN U. S. A.
Library of Congress Catalog Number: 89-64131
ISBN 0-934706-10-7

FOREWORD

For over 30 years readers have been asking *Ceramics Monthly* for solutions to their ceramics problems. The best and the most pertinent of answers to these questions are published each month in the Answers to Questions column.

Many staff members have provided the answers, and when solutions were not available within the resources of the magazine, we consulted outside experts.

Readership surveys have indicated that this column is one of the most widely read sections of *Ceramics Monthly*, and requests for a compendium of past columns have grown steadily. When *Great Ideas for Potters*, a compilation of the best from the *Ceramics Monthly* Suggestions column, was published in 1983, its success convinced us that a similar book based on the Answers to Questions column would help fill an equal need. And, like the columns they are taken from, the "Idea" book is mostly hints on tools and processes; the "Answers" book covers mostly clays and glazes and is more technical. We think the two will complement each other and serve as useful references for ceramists.

Barbara Tipton
Calgary, Alberta

TABLE OF CONTENTS

CLAY

GLAZES

THE STUDIO

CLAY

CERAMIC BODIES

Local Clays

Is it possible to use raw clay found on our own land? What would be the process of preparing it? There is so much here, I think it would be fun to try, but I am not sure just where to begin.

Most clay taken directly from the ground needs some cleaning to remove unwanted materials, and not all clays will work properly. For a preliminary test, after digging the clay, dry it out and hammer it into small pieces or pulverize it. Then put the clay into a bucket and cover with water. Let this mixture stand, stirring occasionally, until you have a slip. Force this slip through a screen (a window screen will do for a first test) to remove undesirable materials such as pebbles, roots, etc. Pour the screened slip onto plaster bats and allow it to stand until enough water has drained off to make the clay of the right consistency.

I have some clay dug locally that has good plasticity and fires to a salmon color at Cone 04. It is extremely porous at this temperature, however, and I wonder if it should be fired higher?

You can determine the maturing range of a clay by running a firing test. Make a series of small "bricks" approximately 1×1×3 inches in dimension. Since you know the clay is quite porous if fired to Cone 04, make the first firing of two test bricks to Cone 02. After they have cooled, break them open and check the porosity. If they still seem quite porous, fire two more to a temperature two or three cones hotter, and keep repeating the procedure until you have found the cone range at which the clay is well matured—but not overfired.

1

I have recently had access to some red clay taken from a river bed which fires successfully to Cone 06. The only difficulty is that it is sticky to handle. Can you tell me what I should add to the clay to make it easier to work?

First, try mixing your clay with another red-firing or buff clay which is not so plastic. Or you may experimentally add kaolin (in 10% increments). According to Michael Cardew in *Pioneer Pottery,* kaolin increases working properties of clay and in small amounts will not weaken the color. In fact, an addition of 10% intensifies it.

We have found a source of clay on our land and would like to use it for pottery. However, the processed clay is very short, and has a tendency to crumble. Can anything be added to or subtracted from the clay to provide a better material for handbuilding?

Try passing the liquid slip through a very fine mesh screen to remove any sand in the clay; if this doesn't give better results, add ball clay or bentonite for greater plasticity. Either one should be added to your clay in its dry state. Additions of bentonite may be at 1–3%; a ball clay addition may be as high as 10%.

I have been digging a natural earthenware which is very plastic, but which tends to crack on drying. I have tried adding sand, but this doesn't seem to solve the problem. Do you have any suggestions for using this clay as part of a body with commercial value?

Add coarse clays, sand or grog, and a substantial quantity of clay with particle size somewhere in between (Cedar Heights Goldart, for example). Having a full range of particle sizes is more likely to result in an all-around, reliable clay body.

Basic Ingredients

Where are the largest deposits of kaolin located?

In the United States the primary deposits are located in Florida, Georgia and South Carolina. Outside this country, there are major deposits in China, Czechoslovakia, England, France, Germany and a number of other countries.

The September 1977 article, "Making Cranks for Production Firing," by George and Nancy Wettlaufer, lists 100-mesh mullite as one of the ingredients in making their refractory casting body. Can you suggest a source for this compound, and tell me what it is?

Mullite is a relatively pure alumina silicate ($3Al_2O_3 \cdot 2SiO_2$) which is extremely refractory. The material is available from a number of ceramic suppliers including Hammill and Gillespie, Inc., Box 104, Livingston, New Jersey 07039.

What is bentonite and why is it used so much?

Bentonite is an extremely plastic natural clay that is derived from volcanic ash. Its chief constituent is montmorillonite ($Al_2O_3 \cdot 5SiO \cdot 7H_2O$). It is mined mostly in Wyoming and South Dakota. Bentonite is added to glaze to help keep the glaze particles in suspension; it is added to "short" clay to give more plasticity. Generally, the addition of 1–3% is adequate. Because bentonite clumps when it is wetted, it should be added dry to other dry ingredients, then these should be stirred together before the water is added.

I've noticed within some recipes published in *Ceramics Monthly* the material "Additive-A" mentioned. Could you tell me what this is?

Additive-A is an aid in improving workability of low-moisture clay bodies with additional higher green and dry strength. It has also been found useful in preventing sulfate scumming and reducing breakage on firing, according to a research and development source at Reed Lignin, Inc., producers of the material. Additive-A is commonly known as calcium lignosulfonate, a 100% soluble brown powder with a pH of 3. See your ceramics supplier for more information.

Recently I read a book on Scandinavian pottery in which many of the illustrations were captioned "thrown chamotte," described further as a mixture of earthenware clay and fired stoneware clay. Do you have any additional information?

Chamotte is the French word for grog, but through

3

its use in Scandinavia, the term has come to mean heavily grogged clay, especially stoneware. Ware thrown or handbuilt with this material is commonly left unglazed to accentuate the surface.

Grog

When I switched from stoneware to porcelain, I found the lack of grog to be quite a problem, particularly when throwing large forms. Is there such a thing as porcelain grog? I haven't seen it advertised under that name.

Porcelain or white grog is sold under the name Molochite. It is available in a wide range of particle sizes. This compound is composed of mullite and amorphous silica, which give it a low thermal expansion. Porcelain grog can also be made by calcining kaolin to Cone 8, grinding and sieving to a suitable particle size.

Recently I attempted to make my own grog by crushing and pulverizing dry greenware scraps, then firing them. The only trouble I have encountered is that there is too much range of size to make the grog useful. Do you have a solution?

In a 1963 *Ceramics Monthly*, Richard Peeler suggested that the fired grog be passed through four different sieves; in this way you end up with four grades of pulverized grog, plus some fired powder. The grog first is placed in a 50-mesh screen, agitated, and all the particles that fall through should be set aside and labeled "calcined clay." This can be used as an addition to clay bodies that are too dense or tight. Next, the grog that didn't pass through the 50-mesh screen is placed in a 30-mesh screen, and the process is repeated to produce a supply of "fine grog." Then, a 14-mesh screen is used to get a "medium grog." Finally, an 8-mesh screen is used to make a "coarse" grade. The remainder, which didn't pass through the 8-mesh, can be labeled as "extra coarse" grog.

What percentage of grog is added to clay to give it a coarse texture?

Try using about 10% grog for wheel work, and from 20 to 40% grog for handbuilding pottery or sculpture. Remember that grog is pre-shrunk and therefore will reduce shrinkage. It also will render a clay less plastic.

Egyptian Paste

We are currently working on establishing a vocational program which would involve the making of Egyptian paste beads. At this point we have all the necessary raw materials for Egyptian paste but lack the funds for investing in a gram scale. Would it be possible to provide a recipe for Egyptian paste that can be measured by volume?

A simply formulated volume recipe for a self-glazing body appeared in the January 1962 issue of *Ceramics Monthly* and is adapted below:

Egyptian Paste (Cone 08–04)

Bicarbonate of Soda	4	teaspoons
Flint	8	tablespoons
Bentonite	8	teaspoons
	20	teaspoons
Add: Copper Carbonate	1	teaspoon

For this recipe, all measurements are level. If the copper carbonate is omitted, the resulting mixture will fire to a creamy white color; with the copper carbonate, the formula has the traditional brilliant blue of Egyptian paste. Two teaspoons of Naples yellow stain added to the white will turn it into a pale yellow; ½ to 1 teaspoon of manganese dioxide will give purple. Other glaze colors may be used and tested to determine the amounts to obtain specific shades.

In preparing the batch, combine the ingredients and sift them together several times or put them through an 80-mesh screen. Add water only when you are ready to work the body, then add just enough to make the mixture the consistency of a thick paste. The batch will thicken rather fast but can be brought back to the right working characteristics by adding a few more drops of water.

Some time ago I purchased some Egyptian paste; now I am having trouble working with it and firing it successfully. The clay itself seems either too sticky or too crum-

bly to work with, and sometimes it has no glaze after the firing. Would you have suggestions for handling this material?

Egyptian paste is just naturally difficult to handle. If you add the water to the clay flour very slowly, you will be able to get just the right consistency between the sticky and crumbly stages. Also, don't overwork or overhandle the paste, or use for long on an absorbent surface, since this may extract the soluble soda. Many potters prefer to use press molds with Egyptian paste because of this restriction. When the work is finished, place it on plastic or some other nonabsorbent surface, or stilt it immediately for firing, and try not to handle it after the clay is dry. The "glaze" is an efflorescence on the surface that may be brushed off if touched.

Flameware and Ovenware

The use of large amounts of spodumene and petalite for making flameware bodies is well documented. But short of making flameware, will small amounts of these materials improve thermal shock resistance? Is the effect in proportion to the amount used? What is the affected temperature range?

Theoretically, small amounts (from 5 to 20%) of spodumene and petalite may make small improvements in thermal shock resistance of clay bodies, provided the appropriate firing temperature of this system is determined. Lithia bodies' resistance to thermal shock is extremely sensitive to firing temperature. Thus, without experimentally determining the appropriate cone range for your specific thermal shock body, you might simply be throwing away dollars spent on spodumene or petalite. The best thermal shock-resistant lithia ceramics are fired to Cone 11 or 12. At Cone 10, some such bodies completely fail basic thermal shock testing. But when fired to the right temperature, it can be said that generally the more lithia mineral, the more thermal shock resistance. Thermal shock-resistant clay bodies tend to contain 35% or more petalite/spodumene.

Our supplier has informed us that ceramic grade spodumene is no longer available, and that the chemical grade is now sold in its place. We use spodumene in an ovenware body, fired at Cone 9 in oxidation. What changes can we expect, and can you provide a comparative analysis?

Ceramics Monthly tested three representative bodies:

Ovenware I (Cone 9)

Spodumene	40 %
Tennessee Ball Clay	60
	100 %

A light peach-colored, high porosity body when ceramic grade spodumene is used; sandy, finely speckled medium tan, average porosity with the chemical grade.

Ovenware II (Cone 9)

Spodumene	30 %
Pyrophyllite	10
Custer Feldspar	10
Cedar Heights Fireclay (12 mesh)	30
Tennessee Ball Clay (7)	20
	100 %
Add: Bentonite	3 %

An off-white, fused body (requires thorough mixing) when ceramic grade spodumene is used; finely speckled sandy tan, fused body with the chemical grade.

Ovenware III (Cone 9)

Spodumene	30 parts
Pyrophyllite	10
Custer Feldspar	10
Kentucky Ball Clay (OM4)	20
Bentonite	2
	72 parts

A pale cream, fused body when ceramic grade spodumene is used; a finely speckled tan, fused body with the chemical grade.

Samples were prepared of each of the bodies—the only variable being the grade of spodumene used. Substantial differences in color were found in all the bodies as well as up to 2% shrinkage change, with variable porosity.

Generally speaking, the chemical grade spodumene bodies were more fused, tended to be somewhat speckled under normal mixing conditions, with significantly darker colorations overall.

A direct substitution of petalite produced results much closer to samples of the old ceramic grade than the new chemical grade spodumene in terms of color, porosity and shrinkage. The effect of petalite, however, was somewhat whiter. For those involved in ovenware usage, our tests suggest that a petalite/spodumene substitution is certainly worth further experimentation.

For purposes of comparison, generalized percent analyses of the two grades of spodumene follow. Ceramic grade: Na_2O–0.35, K_2O–0.60, Li_2O–6.86, CaO and MgO–0.28, Al_2O_3–26.33, SiO_2–64.17, Fe_2O_2–0.90, loss on ignition–0.62. Chemical grade: Na_2O–0.60, K_2O–1.18, Li_2O–5.70, CaO and MgO–not available, Al_2O_3–24.80, SiO_2–63.00, Fe_2O_3–2.00, loss on ignition–not available.

I am interested in producing flameware, but my gas kiln always fires with an uneven temperature from top to bottom. Will this be a problem in making ware of this type, provided I properly formulate the body?

Firing temperature can be important if flameware bodies derive their heat shock resistance from lithium. Variations from the intended maturation point may signal a problem with resistance to cracking, and may make the ware hazardous for stovetop use.

I would like to use my clay for making ovenware. There is much information available concerning the minerals that decrease clay breakage from thermal shock, but nothing describing a simple test and standards for evaluating such a test of the clay body. Can you help?

F. H. Norton in his text, *Fine Ceramics, Technology and Applications*, lists the following requirements for ovenware: "Withstand quenching in cold water from 150°C; have a smooth, hard, noncrazing surface to withstand abrasion and the usual cleaners; be capable of holding durable decorations; have reasonable mechanical strength."

What are the requirements for low-fire pottery that can be used in the oven? Is it primarily a matter of the clay or glaze?

Red clays that are rather coarse grained work well. This enables the ware to better withstand the repeated shock of heating and cooling. Any glaze will work satisfactorily as long as it is matched to the body and does not develop crazing.

Microwave Ware

I would appreciate a comment on the subject of pottery in the microwave oven. Are lustered pots as harmful to the oven as metal containers? What testing is appropriate before I can assure customers that my ware is "microwave safe"?

Ceramics Monthly wrote Dan R. McConnell, then senior product manager for Amana Refrigeration, Inc. He responded: "The use of metal containers [in microwave ovens] is generally forbidden because the large metallic surface area prevents the absorption of the microwave energy by the food, and acts essentially as a shield. The reflected microwave energy travels back to the magnetron tube causing the tube to overheat, which in turn results in long-term degradation and reduction in life [of the tube]. Only rarely is an instantaneous failure of the tube caused by the use of metal containers. Because of the subtle long-term effects on the tube, there is a great deal of confusion about the use of metal containers.

"In general, ceramics make excellent containers in the use of microwave ovens. Ceramics absorb very little microwave energy and therefore do not heat up themselves. They permit the microwave energy to penetrate to the food. There is very little, if any, reflection as in the case of metals.

"The small amount of metal in [typical] glazes appears to have no significant effect on the usability of the ceramic container. There is no significant difference in reflection of microwave energy nor in heating effect; therefore, glazes present no problem in the operation of the microwave oven and cause no damage."

Exceptions to Dan McConnell's conclusions are metallic glazes such as commercial lusters and reduced metallic raku. All such metallics should be avoided for microwave use.

I want to make microwave ware, and am wondering if there is an easy method of determining whether my pots are suitable. Are there other special considerations in producing ceramic forms for the microwave oven?

According to an article in *Ceramic Industry* magazine, the potter may test clay bodies and glazes by placing a fired work in the microwave oven along with a separate cup of water (in a glass container); turn the oven on high for one minute. To be safe for microwave use, the pot should feel cool and the water warm after this cooking. If the water is cool and the pot is warm, the latter is absorbing microwave energy and thus should not be used in such equipment.

Generally speaking, unsuitable ware contains metal, either in the form of luster, heavily reduced oxides such as those found in some raku ware, or fuming (a selectively placed thin layer of tin chloride fuming, however, is used to create the extremely hot area on microwave browning pans).

Thrown ware or other circular forms should prove ideal for microwave use—they have an advantage over square and oblong shapes in that forms with corners tend to cook unevenly. You might consider producing shapes with a central tube—similar to an angelfood cake pan—eliminating entirely the slower-cooking center. Avoid hollow handles or a porous clay body because these can trap water which gets excessively hot in the microwave.

Casting Bodies

I have followed the instructions from "Making Cranks for Production Firing" in the September 1977 issue, and am unable to make things work successfully. The cranks crack in the drying stage, and the clay doesn't release from the molds. I have departed from the instructions by substituting Kentucky ball clay for the C&C ball clay mentioned in the recipe.

Within the ranges specified, I am mixing 50% mullite, 22.5% talc, and 27.5% ball clay, adding water to the consistency of cream. The casting begins to crack soon after I've poured it into the mold. Could it be that the sides of the plaster form are too steep?

The article's authors, George and Nancy Wettlaufer, reply: "It would be helpful to have a little more information, but the most probable cause of the cracking is excessive deflocculation; this is especially true if you are not experienced in working with slip. We assume that the mold is smooth and of correct density, that you have made the two or three break-in castings which are usually necessary, and that you did in fact deflocculate the slip (since cracking may also result from not deflocculating at all).

"Small changes in material compositions can make a big difference in the characteristics and stability of casting slip, and such changes affect the amount of deflocculant needed. For example, California talc—your probable source—can have as much as four times the soluble sodium salts as the New York talc we use. Some Kentucky ball clays have high soluble salts (0.25%), others are low in such salts. C&C ball clay, which we use, has about 0.08%—thus substitutions of talc and ball clay as mentioned in the previous examples would dictate the need for much less deflocculant for the same results as given in the *Ceramics Monthly* formula.

"In trying to determine whether your slip is over deflocculated, look for the following signs: the casting will be gritty in the top portions where slip is drained from the mold; the form will cast too slowly—you should get a ⅜-inch wall thickness in ½ to ¾ hour with typical plaster density; the slip will form a skin across the top in two hours or less; and finally (as mentioned previously), the castings will stick to the mold.

"If you will make up a small test mold and mix test slip batches with ½ and ¼ of the original deflocculant mix, the test castings should give a solution to the cracking problem. Slips are tricky at best, sometimes affected by small changes in materials. Consistent testing will require continual attention to details."

In order to combine slip-cast and thrown parts in the regular production of porcelain tableware, is it possible to use the same body for both slip and throwing clay?

Some porcelains are ideal for use as both slip and throwing clay, being plastic enough for wheel work, yet sufficiently deflocculated (with a greater concentration of suspended body solids) for slip casting. The best multipurpose porcelains contain natural quantities of deflocculating materials such as feldspar or sodium compounds, organic fermentation or ball clay. Many typical formulations will qualify for such use—simply cast a few throwing bodies to determine which performs best.

I am interested in casting red clay flowerpots as surfaces for a variety of decorative techniques. Can you recommend a casting formula?

Cedar Heights Clay Company offers the following batch recipe for general casting of red earthenware:

Red Clay Casting Body (Cone 04–1)

Cedar Heights Redart Clay	69.20 %
Water	30.80
	100.00 %
Add: Soda Ash	0.14 %
"N" Brand Sodium Silicate	0.64 %

This casting slip has a specific gravity of 1.75, dry shrinkage of approximately 6%, total shrinkage after firing of approximately 9% at Cone 04 and 14% at Cone 1.

Why do I have trouble casting satisfactorily with a red-firing clay? I have tried clays from local deposits as well as prepared commercial red clays.

There are inherent impurities or at least chemical differences in all natural red-burning clays which make them difficult to deflocculate and cast properly. Most red clays can be deflocculated to a degree using one or more deflocculants such as sodium silicate, Calgon, or one of the phosphates. The type or amount to use for best results is a matter of experimentation. You will find that larger percentages of both deflocculant and water will be necessary than with most white casting bodies.

12

Our studio has been trying to develop a casting slip based on local clay, but no matter how hard we try, it will not deflocculate. Is there some method we could use?

Some slips simply will not deflocculate—the cause is too much free alkali (lithium, potassium, sodium). Perhaps your local clay could be used in smaller quantities within a larger slip recipe. Sometimes substantially smaller quantities of such clays will produce the desired deflocculation in an otherwise flocculated slip.

I am experimenting with making my own casting slip and currently have one that contains about ⅓ of its weight in water. This seems insufficiently deflocculated. What is a reasonable goal for water content in slip?

A good casting slip may contain as little as 25% water (by weight). This is achieved by proper deflocculation with electrolytes such as soda ash or sodium silicate in amounts from approximately 0.3% to 0.5% by weight. Usually both sodium silicate and soda ash are used in the slip recipe, and a good starting point is equal parts of each. Some clays, however, will not deflocculate sufficiently to make good slip. If yours seems resistant to further deflocculation, you may wish to try another clay base. Many handbuilding or throwing bodies make fine casting slips when properly deflocculated, and any of these are worth experimenting with.

We have been involved with quite a bit of casting over the past few months, but recently the slip has been impossible to deflocculate. There has been no change in our recipe nor in the materials, so this problem really has us baffled. How can we get our slip back to normal?

The one material which is the most common culprit whenever there are major changes in casting slip is the water, which may vary greatly in mineral content. To determine if your water is at fault, substitute distilled water in an experimental batch. If this makes deflocculation possible again, then you may want to switch to distilled water to permanently eliminate this problem, or substitute distilled water for part of the local water content.

I have been searching for a suitable recipe which might have application as a Cone 10 stoneware or whiteware casting body. Do you have any suggestions?

The following body is suitable for use at Cone 10; it fires off-white in oxidation, and gray in reduction:

High-Fire Casting Body (Cone 7–10)

Potash Feldspar	20.0 %
Kaolin	27.0
Kentucky Ball Clay (OM 4)	17.2
Cedar Heights Goldart	17.5
Sodium Silicate (dry)	0.3
Flint	18.0
	100.0 %

What is the best way to color a white casting slip? Will adding a color change the casting behavior of the slip?

Any ceramic colorant can be added to a slip. These include any of the coloring oxides or carbonates (iron, cobalt, manganese, etc.) and commercially prepared body stains and underglazes. If a dry color is added you should ball mill the slip to get a homogeneous color. By merely stirring in the colorant, you will get a speckled or mottled effect. To eliminate the need for ball milling, add liquid underglaze, which will be completely dispersed if stirred sufficiently.

The addition of colorant should not change the casting properties of the slip.

RECIPES

Porcelain

I am interested in the formulation of Chinese porcelain, and have seen reference to the use of *kao-ling* and *petuntse*. Can you identify these materials in contemporary terms?

In the British magazine *Pottery Quarterly*, Nigel Wood presents some new research in this regard: "Chinese porcelain is probably the most misunderstood ceramic material of all time and the few remarks on its manufacture that are found in almost all the books can be summed up more or less as follows:

'Chinese porcelain is made from equal parts of kaolin and petuntse (feldspar). Both materials derive from decomposed granites and are like our own China clays and Cornish stones (respectively). The porcelain clay is aged for years before being used, and after forming is given a long firing to about 1400°C.'

"When one starts to dig deeper into the subject one soon realizes that these much-repeated 'facts' are wrong in virtually every detail. Chinese porcelain is nowhere near as close to European hard pastes as the books suggest; feldspar is not the major flux used in the body as it is with Western porcelain; and the decomposition of granite is not the process that created petuntse. In fact, the true nature of Chinese porcelain is so different from how it is usually presented that an accurate description of the material would have to read as follows: 'Chinese porcelain is made from at least three parts of petuntse to two of kaolin. Petuntse derives from volcanic rock and is very different from Cornish stone. The porcelain clay is used soon after being prepared and is fired quickly to about 1300°C.'

"To this can be added what is probably the most important fact of all about Chinese porcelain: potash mica rather than feldspar is the major flux in the body, and where feldspar is present in Chinese porcelain, it is usually of the soda rather than the potash type."

I was impressed with the article "Three Northwest Potters" (April 1981), and am wondering if you can tell me what body Tom Coleman uses?

For thrown and altered ware, Tom employed the following recipe (in parts by weight):

Translucent Porcelain Body
(Cone 11, oxidation or reduction)

Pyrophyllite	5 parts
Custer Feldspar	47
Grolleg Kaolin	50
Flint (200 Mesh)	35
Bentonite	5
Veegum T	1
	143 parts

Can you provide a recipe for bone china, and tell me something about its origins? Is it the same as porcelain?

Bone china was perfected in England by Josiah Spode (1754–1827) who used the ash from burnt animal bones to flux what we today would call Cornwall stone and kaolin. Records show his recipe was:

Spode Bone China (Cone 6)

Bone Ash	52 %
Cornish Stone	24
China Clay	24
	100 %

If you want to make Spode's bone china, substitute an English kaolin such as Grolleg for the china clay, Cornwall stone for Cornish stone. Bone china is fired to a nearly self-glazed state in saggars filled with sand to preserve the china shape unwarped. Then glaze is applied after the high-temperature bisque firing, and the work usually is refired (glaze) in the low-fire range, where warping will not occur.

Bone china is porcelain, or a relative of porcelain (depending on whom you talk to). Compare it with the following porcelain recipe:

True Porcelain Body (Cone 8)

Kona F-4 Feldspar	30 %
Grolleg Kaolin	40
Tennessee Ball Clay (7 or 10)	10
Flint	20
	100 %

While both these clay bodies contain kaolin as their core, the bone china body will require additional plasticizers like Macaloid in order to be useful for handbuilding or throwing, whereas the porcelain body, after suitable aging, will be useful for any ceramic forming process. Both these clays can be cast with a typical addition of small amounts of sodium silicate and soda ash for deflocculation.

Recent studies of historic bone china have led me to an appreciation of the medium which now I would like to try. Could you suggest a suitable body which might be used as a starting point?

You might consider trying the following:

Bone China Body (Cone 9)

Bone Ash	50 %
Kaolin	25
Flint	25
	100 %

Nylon fibers may be mixed with this clay to increase workability in handbuilding, and plasticity may be improved, if desired, by the addition of a few percentages of Macaloid. Forms may need to be supported in bisque molds, or with sand during firing, which should include a 15-minute soak at peak temperature.

I am interested in Parian, a soft-paste porcelain. What ingredients might be used to mix it?

Parian ware, according to Richard Behrens's handbook, *Glaze Projects*, can be produced with a clay body of 30% Tennessee ball clay, 64% nepheline syenite, and 6% bentonite. This body should have adequate workability for throwing or handbuilding, and should fire to Cone 4.

Salt-Glaze Bodies

Do you know a recipe for a salt-glaze body producing those nice reds and oranges in reduction? I want something in the traditional high-fire salt range, but with a coarse texture.

The following body is a colorful one, producing strong orange-yellow and iron reds in reduction when salt fired. It also contains a substantial amount of grog for a coarse surface.

Salt-Glaze Stoneware Clay Body (Cone 8–11)

Cedar Heights Goldart Clay	50 %
Ball Clay (C&C)	20
Grog (20 mesh)	30
	100 %

This body can also be fired in regular reduction kilns, or in oxidation with typical changes in color for these atmospheres.

I am searching for an almost-white clay body for use in high-fire salt glazing. Will you recommend one?

The following body recipe should meet your requirements, is good for throwing and handbuilding, and will be very light when salt glazed, even if reduced.

Off-White Salt-Glaze Body

(Cone 9, oxidation or reduction)

Kona F-4 Feldspar	15	parts
Ball Clay (C&C)	20	
Cedar Heights Bonding Clay	20	
Cedar Heights Fireclay	25	
Flint	10	
	90	parts
Add: Porcelain Grog (Molochite)	10	parts

This recipe is especially good with oxide washes for color: mix oxides with a little flint and a pinch of salt to encourage glassiness over the decoration.

Medium-Temperature Bodies

Can you provide a recipe which gives a toasty brown clay body when fired in oxidation between Cones 5 and 7?

Try equal parts (by weight) of A.P. Green fireclay, Cedar Heights Redart clay and ball clay, fired in oxidation.

Do you have a recipe for a dark brown clay body, suitable for throwing or handbuilding, which fires at Cone 4 in oxidation?

Try the following toasty brown body:

Brown Clay Body (Cone 4)

A.P. Green Fireclay	45.0	parts
Cedar Heights Redart Clay	20.0	
C&C Ball Clay	5.0	
Kingman Feldspar	5.0	
Burnt Umber	1.5	
Fine Grog (optional)	12.0	
	88.5	parts

This body shrinks 12% or less depending on the amount of grog added.

Slips and Engobes

I would like to locate a recipe for white slip which would fit my stoneware clay body, even when applied thickly. What do you suggest?

Minnesota potter Warren MacKenzie commented that there really is no reason for thick slips to be complicated. A line blend of kaolin and ball clay ought to produce slips to fit any clay. To find a good fit for your stoneware body, try a line blend of Georgia kaolin (6 Tile) and Kentucky ball clay (OM 4) in 10% increments: 90% kaolin and 10% ball clay; 80% kaolin, 20% ball clay; etc.

I'm interested in locating an inexpensive and easily formulated white slip for use on stoneware at Cone 9, in reduction and salt. Can you offer any suggestions?

Try using typical kiln wash (50% kaolin and 50% flint) as a good white slip. This means one less batch to make up for production use. It fires hard on ware and provides good color under glaze.

Could you recommend a black, vitreous slip for Cone 9 firing?

The following recipe may be of interest:

Black Vitreous Slip (Cone 9)

Whiting	10 %
Nepheline Syenite	15
Kaolin (ASP 400)	20
Tennessee Ball Clay (1)	30
Flint	25
	100 %
Add: Red Iron Oxide	3 %
Manganese Dioxide	2 %

This slip has a variety of applications when single firing ware—for sgraffito decoration, under glaze or alone.

I would like to have similar slip recipes for use on bisque and on ware during its various stages of drying. What would you suggest?

Parameters of slip for decoration usually fall within the following guidelines (expressed in parts by weight):

for leather-hard ware, mix one part ball clay with 2.5 to 6.5 parts kaolin; for bone dry or bisqueware, mix one part ball clay with from 1.5 to 2.5 parts kaolin. If you prefer a fluxed slip, add 0.5 parts nepheline syenite or feldspar to the slips for use at stoneware ranges. It may require 0.3 parts of any boron frit to flux a low-fire slip. Add colorant oxides or carbonates according to decorative requirements.

FORMULATING CHANGES

Adding Color and Texture to Clays

While my electric kiln is located in an area with very minimal ventilation, I nevertheless wish to make sculpture with large amounts of burnout material in an unglazed Cone 9 clay body. Are there any such materials which do not give off smoke or fumes?

Coarsely ground perlite is suitable as a burnout-type material in ceramic objects. Instead of actually burning out, perlite generally melts out around Cone 8 (depending on clay body composition), exercising a very mild fluxing action on the clay, and leaving only small pockets where the coarse particles were originally located. Usually there is no glassy appearance, since the small amount of flux is absorbed by the body. Below the high-fire range, perlite leaves a coarse texture similar to the effects of burnout material; throughout the firing range, perlite generally melts when contacting glaze. Characterized as an expanded volcanic glass, perlite may reduce the need for kiln ventilation compared to combustible materials, but it is essential that all electric kilns be adequately ventilated to remove fumes from metallic fluxes, colorants, sulfur and carbonaceous gases usually present in clay and glazes.

I am using a clay which fires light to dark brown in reduction and would like to have dark specks in the body. What do you suggest?

There are two materials that you might consider

using—granular ilmenite and granular manganese. The latter will provide a strong, dark brown speck, while the former will give a peppery appearance. Try these materials in a 20- to 40-mesh size, and use them in small amounts according to your preference.

Is it possible to obtain the iron-flecked results usually seen on stoneware in the earthenware range; if so, how?

A dark-flecked appearance could be obtained in a light-firing, low-fire body by wedging into it some coarse-ground manganese dioxide. Using light-color glazes would further enhance the iron-flecked appearance.

I have seen some warm, toasty looking clay bodies purported to have been fired only in oxidation. They appear to have all the rich orange-brown color associated with the best reduction firing. What is the secret?

There really is no secret since the information has been available for years in the technical literature of the field. Spodumene is the usual "colorant," typically added in a relatively large quantity (20–30% of the dry clay batch). Since this addition has no plasticity of its own, ball clay, bentonite or synthetic plasticizers are often found in larger than usual quantities for throwing or handbuilding bodies. Spodumene is a lithium compound with negative thermal expansion; therefore it tends to affect glaze fit, requiring adjustments in most typical recipes to prevent crazing.

I recently tried adding manganese dioxide to my stoneware clay to give a brown body color, but have run into trouble. I am getting a beautiful dark brown color, but something else, too. Some of the thinner pieces have been slumping and sagging out of shape. Is it possible that a 3% addition of manganese could be causing the trouble?

Very possible, indeed. Manganese dioxide is a rather strong fluxing agent. With the 3% addition, you may find it necessary to lower the firing temperature of your stoneware clay. Try running a series of firing tests to ascertain the best firing temperature for your particular clay.

I make handbuilt pots from colored and uncolored clays and fire them to Cone 6. However, when colorants like cobalt carbonate are added to the wet clay body, there is little or no difference in appearance. Is there anything which will differentiate the colored and uncolored bodies when I'm working with them, but which will burn out in firing?

Several possible stains could be added to the wet clay and could even be so mixed as to approximate the fired color. These include ink, poster paint or any nonpermanent water-base dye. Although some contain materials which might affect the final color, a test firing will determine results with specific brands.

Lowering Firing Temperatures

What can I add to a Cone 01 clay to bring its maturing point down to around Cone 06?

There are many raw materials which would act as a flux when mixed with your Cone 01 clay, such as talc or various frits. Try making a series of test bodies by adding talc or frit to your dry clay in 5% increments. After adding water to your batches and wedging, roll out some small slabs or other simple shapes, and fire. This preliminary testing will give you the approximate amount of the particular flux needed. More careful experimenting, checking for raw and fired properties, should then be made before you attempt a large batch.

I want to lower the firing temperature of a stoneware body from Cone 10 to Cone 6. What would be a good single addition for this purpose?

Nepheline syenite is a reasonable choice for lowering the maturing temperature of stoneware. Start by using it as a replacement for any feldspar already present in the body recipe, or make small test batches with nepheline syenite added in 5% increments. However, it may be necessary to include ball clay, bentonite or a synthetic plasticizer to offset the loss of plasticity caused by the nepheline syenite addition.

I have heard of using nepheline syenite for lowering the

maturing temperature of stoneware. Can whiting also be used?

There are many materials which are useful for lowering stoneware maturing temperatures, and whiting is among them. This flux is commonly used in the production of bone china. It adds hardness to the body, but bleaches iron. However, care should be taken with whiting and other flux additions (such as bone ash and talc) to clay bodies. Many are sudden melters, and overfiring by as little as two cones might mean the difference between a mature clay body and a puddle on the kiln shelf.

Absorption

As a studio potter, I sell vitreous stoneware, the usual mix of decorative works and functional pieces, including tableware. At a recent art fair another potter challenged my description of the work as vitreous, commenting that the fact it holds water is not sufficient. I'm wondering if there is an official standard for vitreous ware and if my work qualifies?

U.S. Government standards state that ware is vitreous when demonstrating an absorption of less than 0.5%. Much stoneware produced by studio potters does not qualify and instead might be classed as semivitreous. According to Daniel Rhodes in his book *Stoneware and Porcelain,* an absorbency of 2 or 3% is not objectionable for ware intended to contain food or liquid. However, sanitary ware should have an absorption of 1% or less.

A simple test for percentage of absorption involves forming clay bars (Rhodes recommends at least three), each 5×5×10 cm. Fire the bars, weigh them to the nearest centigram, then boil them for two hours. Dry the bars to remove surface water, and weigh them again to the nearest centigram. The percentage of absorption is equal to:

Boiled weight – Dry weight ÷ Dry Weight × 100

I fire at Cone 6–7 in oxidation, using a body which consists of 33% each of A.P. Green fireclay, Kentucky ball clay (OM 4), and Cedar Heights Redart. To that is added from 10–15% silica sand and/or grog. I have noticed leakage through tea cups or planter saucers of this body. Would that much grog or sand be a factor?

I have also noticed that the body chips more easily than commercially manufactured ware. What will make it more resistant to leakage and chipping, yet maintain the same color and temperature for firing?

A fine, vitreous body in the Cone 6–7 range may be produced with adaptations to the clay you mentioned. From 10 to 15% silica sand or grog is sometimes sufficient to open the body, conducting water through a network of capillaries which such additions create. Thus the first step is to remove this addition and test for leakage.

But there are excellent vitreous clay bodies which contain sizable amounts of grog or sand balanced with compounds which tend to have a fluxing action. One solution would be to experimentally add nepheline syenite in 5% increments (from 5 to 30%). Since this decreases plasticity, more ball clay may be needed to increase that loss through this "short" addition.

Plasticity

Our local supplier no longer is able to stock Macaloid, which we use as a plasticizer in porcelain. Can you recommend a substitute for this material?

Veegum T may be directly substituted for Macaloid.

We are currently formulating a clay body which is relatively nonplastic even though the materials employed are of small particle sizes. I thought particle size and plasticity were directly related. What's the problem here?

Generally speaking, plasticity and fine particle size are directly related, but there are exceptions. Some clays with a high flint content are never very plastic, regardless of the particle size employed.

TROUBLESHOOTING

Body Defects

We have just begun using a Cone 6 porcelain in our busy teaching studio and are having a problem with tiny particles of hard clay that show up when the porcelain is reconditioned.

Our reconditioning process is this: After the students rewedge any usable clay at the end of class, soft, thrown scrap goes back into one barrel, hard trimmings and greenware are broken up and go into a second barrel to which water is added. When both barrels are of a uniform softness, we pour off the excess water and lay out the contents on a plaster table until the batch returns to throwing consistency. What are we doing wrong?

Your processing of the soft scrap sounds fine and may be continued, provided there are no hard lumps in that batch, but we recommend a change in the method of handling hard trimmings and greenware. Such scraps slake more consistently when first allowed to become completely dry. When dry, break them up in small pieces and sift them into a barrel of water. Water temperature will greatly affect the speed and completeness of slaking—hot water is preferred to cold.

These processing techniques should be sufficient for nearly all porcelain bodies, but if yours continues to be plagued with hard clay particles, then it is recommended that all scrap be reduced not just to the slaked state, but be mixed with sufficient water to produce slip which is then dried on plaster until it reaches good working consistency.

I mix clay from slurry, let it set overnight, then drain the excess water before drying the clay on bats. Occasionally the slip has deflocculated: it runs off my fingers in streams—great for casting, but unthrowable after drying. Can anything be added to the slip to flocculate it?

Deflocculation of your clay body could be a result of alkalies in the ingredients or soluble salts in the water. Try adding a small amount of vinegar or calcium chloride (from 0.5–1% of dry ingredients by weight) to the water before mixing your clay.

I have been wet mixing a clay body which contains talc, and have been getting results which suggest that the material does not mix well. Could there be something wrong with the talc which I bought from my local supplier?

Potters' materials are generally industrial grade, produced under sufficient quality control to insure a high standard of consistency. Thus, the potter is advised to first look at the characteristics of the material itself and the studio processes for sources of a problem, since it is more likely that the difficulty originates there.

Talc is a finely ground compound (hydrated magnesium silicate) which normally is not easily mixed with water. When using talc in clay or glazes, it is advisable to mix the ingredients in the dry state before adding water. Talc bodies which are not dry mixed may exhibit uneven properties because of variable concentrations of the talc throughout the batch.

I was advised to add some bentonite to my clay to make it more plastic, but I ended up with a gooey glob of unmanageable mess. Was the advice given me bad, or is there something more I should know about handling this material?

Bentonite is an excellent material for use in increasing the plasticity of clay. Just a small amount is all that is needed—1 to 2%. Your trouble probably came about from trying to add bentonite to moist clay. Because it is so extremely plastic, it must be added dry to the dry clay. These materials should be mixed together intimately before adding water to the batch.

I have several ideas for pieces which will require a separate clay support for firing to Cone 9–10 reduction. Could you please suggest a formula for a body which could handle repeat firings without warpage or cracking?

The best support for any ceramic object is one formed from the same body, as it will shrink and otherwise react to the heat of firing in the same manner as the desired work. Thereafter, such a support is usually discarded. This is the time-tested method commonly used in industry, even when large whiteware pieces are single fired through a great deal of shrinkage. Nevertheless, when shrinkage is not a major consideration, there are instances where repeatedly firing work on the same support can save time. Some potters invert planters over dome-topped bottle/vase-shaped supports in order to glaze fire the bottom. Such props are best made of the most refractory clays for minimum warpage. Thus, bodies such as those suggested in Lowell Baker's article, "Castable Refractories," (November 1981 *Ceramics Monthly*) make good prospects for durable supports. If your work requires that supports be thrown or handbuilt beyond the ability of the more refractory bodies, saggar clay (or any fireclay) will suffice, or simply fire your standard clay body repeatedly.

Firing Defects

Adhesion

I am having difficulty firing lidded jars made from a heavily speckled clay body. It seems that the iron particles pop out and adhere the lid to the jar. Is there an answer to this problem?

Fusing from iron pops can be avoided by painting the lip or flange of the jar with a wash of alumina hydrate. After firing, rinse away the remaining powder. Applying a paste of carborundum grit, or extra fine silica carbide and water, to the lid and twisting it back and forth on the pot will help smooth away any roughness from iron pops.

When I unload my salt kiln, there inevitably is a pot or two that sticks to the shelf, no matter what I use to separate the ware from it. I have been trying to lightly strike the pot a number of times with a wood mallet, but the breakage rate is high. Can you suggest a solution?

Gently strike the shelf around the pot with the wood mallet, keeping moderate pressure on the ware with your free hand. Never hit the ware because it is almost always weaker than the shelf. If you persist, you should be able to remove the ware without breaking the shelf or the pot.

Bloating

Recently my clay body has been bloating as if there were a bubble within the clay wall, while previously it has been perfect in every respect. Can you give some reasons why this might happen?

Bloating may well be one of the most frustrating and difficult clay body defects because of the many probable causes, and because it appears in the final firing with rarely acceptable results. While bloating is commonly associated with excessive reduction, particularly in the early stages of the glaze firing, it is also classically linked to high iron content and too rapid firing. With the current interest in hybrid bodies, much of the potter's bloating may result from insufficient mixing of materials in the clay, such as feldspar, nepheline syenite or colorants. The "bad batch" of clay is unavoidable in bulk processing, even though manufacturers make every effort to avoid mining defective materials.

About the only method for establishing the cause of a specific bloating problem is through an experimental process of elimination by changing firing procedures and body materials until bloating ceases.

Recently I have been plagued with sporadic bloating in my Cone 9 oxidation stoneware clay body (50 parts Goldart, 30 fireclay, 10 ball clay, 10 Custer feldspar and 2 red iron oxide). I've heard that sulfur might be the problem, but I've used this body for years without difficulties; it throws well and has an attractive fired color. Can you suggest ways I might prevent bloating and thus continue with the same clay recipe?

The sulfur content in Goldart (as well as in other Ohio clays) varies, due to its proximity to coal seams which run next to the clay deposits. Many potters have reported continual success with sulfur-bearing clays by firing slowly in the initial stages for both bisque and glaze, taking at least five hours to reach dull red heat before turning the kiln on high, or soaking for 30 minutes with temperature around Cone 08. Other suggestions include keeping the electric kiln vented throughout the firing cycle, and never firing above Cone 9. You might also try opening the body with 5–10% medium grog.

Cracking and Repairing

When I fire large, heavy works, and especially those with large bottom areas, they often warp. Sometimes the slab-built objects crack, even though they have been well made. Can the weight of the piece be the cause? If so, what can I do to prevent this?

The weight of the objects and the size of the base often cause works to deform or crack apart at the seams. Try firing such forms on a thin layer of pure white sand or ground, porous firebrick on the kiln shelves. The granules will act as "rollers" and allow the work to slide as it shrinks.

I need a formula for making a mender for both bisque and greenware.

You will probably have to experiment a bit. Sodium silicate (commonly called waterglass) is one of the most-used mending agents. This would work best on bisqueware either by itself or in combination with slip. For greenware, heavy slip is generally sufficient although small additions of waterglass might help there, too.

I recently came across a reference to a "bisque stick" for mending hairline cracks in bisqueware, but there was no explanation of what this was or where it can be obtained.

This is something you can make for yourself from the same clay you are using for your pottery. Roll out a medium-size coil of the clay, then cut it into several short lengths. When the clay is dry, put it in the kiln and bisque fire it to a very low temperature (about Cone 019). When this bisque crayon is drawn across a hairline crack, the soft bisque will pack readily into the line. When it is glazed, the repair should be unnoticeable.

When Adelaide Robineau's "Scarab Vase" cracked in bisque firing, it was repaired and refired and emerged in

perfect shape. Do you have any idea how this was accomplished? The only information about porcelain repairing I can find says to fill cracks with epoxy after decorating. Such a method is not acceptable to me.

According to an account in Samuel Robineau's memoirs, as related in the book, *Adelaide Alsop Robineau: Glory in Porcelain,* by Peg Weiss, the base of the "Scarab Vase" emerged from the first firing badly cracked. French ceramist Taxile Doat, at the time an associate of Adelaide Robineau at the Academy of Fine Arts, University City (Missouri), advised filling the cracks with paste (low-fire, fritted porcelain), then using (overglaze) enamel to match the glaze. But Adelaide said she would "'either repair the vase at high fire or throw it in the ash can.'" Samuel wrote that "she spent hours filling the cracks with ground [fired] porcelain," glazed the base with the same recipe used on the body of the vase, and after the second firing, the cracks were no longer visible.

A popular method of repairing porcelain today is to force porcelain grog, or Molochite, into the cracks. (Refiring at bisque temperatures may be advisable to check the success of the repair.) The work may then be glazed and fired as usual.

Dunting

Why does porcelain sometimes break in the kiln on the second firing?

If ware is going to crack, the crack usually will appear in the first firing. Perhaps the cracks were imperceptible in the bisque and were accentuated in the glaze firing. It also is possible to crack the object by a too rapid rise in temperature during firing or a too rapid cooling. In either case, slow the firing or cooling process. Avoid turning off all switches or burners at once at maturity; allow a soaking period by lowering or reversing the heat at the end of the firing.

I have been having some very peculiar results in using an alkaline glaze that I compound from a formula that was given to me. When this glaze was used on greenware for once-fire work, the ware broke after it had cooled. I don't

have this trouble when I use the glaze on bisque, but the glaze surface is rough textured. I have seen the glaze used by others and know that the formula is a good one. Do you have any comments on this situation?

Alkalines are extremely soluble. If they are absorbed into the raw clay, they may cause the ware to crack. This is due to the extreme expansion and contraction that alkalines undergo on firing and cooling. If your ware is bisqued soft, the solubility of the alkalines may account for the incomplete glaze surface. Try bisque firing a bit harder, or use a frit to obtain the alkalines in an insoluble form.

Why do works break in the kiln—sometimes before I open it and sometimes months later? I fire to Cone 10 most of the time. The clay is native clay dug near Clayton, Washington, processed and mixed in 2-ton batches. I've used several types of the same glazes for years. My 27-cubic-foot kiln is gas fired, and until recently I've had only about ten objects break in the last four years out of about 1400. My last two firings had 41 pieces in them. Fourteen tall vases and four bowls were broken when I unbricked the door. Some cracks ran the full length and some ran around the forms. I always reduce heavily for ½ hour when the temperature is about 1600°F, then again when the last cone has gone over. It takes ten hours. Then I close the vents and leave it for 24 hours until the temperature is down to 200° or 300°F before opening. I understand it's possible that some glaze doesn't fit the clay and I guess this can cause cracking. In my last two firings some of the unbroken pieces had the same glaze as the broken ones. What do I add or subtract from a glaze to make it fit a certain clay? Do some clays break of their own accord regardless of what glaze is on them? And what can be added to clay to eliminate this? Will too heavy a reduction cause cracking? I feel that I'm reducing all the time and perhaps I don't need to reduce heavily at certain periods.

There are so many variables that it is impossible to provide exact answers, but here are some ideas to work on, all relating to the problem of cracked ware.

If there is any indication of carbonization (black coring) in the cracked wall section, your clay may be too high in iron for reduction, or the reduction may be too heavy. If your clay is high in silica, this may be a cause of breakage due to thermal shock. You may be bisque firing too low for the amount of reduction you do. Are your inside and outside glazes compatible? Are they both alkaline, or both something else? And could the broken pieces have too much glaze on the inside and thus set up unequal stress? These are just suggestions for exploration, and will involve experimentation on your part.

During a recent firing, my forced-air kiln was subjected to a power outage which lasted for about three hours. Because the cones were committed, I decided to cool the kiln, put in new cones, and begin the gas firing again in a typical manner. But on opening the door when the kiln was cool, I found that a high percentage of the ware had broken. This has never happened before, and I can't figure out why it should have happened simply because of a false start and power failure. I earn my living from making pots, and it's important for me to understand this so that it doesn't happen again. Any help you can provide would be appreciated.

There are a few possible answers to the problem you've experienced, but the most logical one is that your kiln lost power very close to a quartz inversion temperature. It is unlikely you will experience this problem again, as even if your kiln loses power during another firing, the odds are against it doing so at a point close to quartz inversion. Technically speaking, the shattering results from an uneven and drastic change in the linear expansion of quartz and other free silica in the body. This expansion may be as much as 1% of the ware's various dimensions in addition to the normal expansion of silica and the other clay materials. It's a good idea to avoid fast changes in temperature when the pyrometer indicates the kiln temperature is in the vicinity of 1058°F (570°C) and 1922°F (1050°C), where quartz inversion takes place. Avoiding these changes will undoubtedly prevent major shattering in the future.

We've just finished our yearly raku workshop, but are disappointed by the number of cracked objects. The clay body we used was:

Raku Clay Body

Talc	30 %
Pyrax	8
A.P. Green Fireclay	19
Kentucky Ball Clay (OM 4)	38
Bentonite	5
	100 %
Add: Silica Sand	6 %

This body throws well and has a whiteness that works nicely with our glazes. Could it be altered to keep its good qualities yet reduce thermal cracking? If this is not a basically sound recipe, could you recommend a body that bisque fires white, is suitable for wheel work and handbuilding, is not excessively abrasive when throwing and has good thermal shock resistance?

Your recipe seems to be a variation of the classic ball clay/talc low-fire body with an addition of fireclay for more openness and workability, Pyrax (pyrophyllite) and sand to resist thermal shock. Though the talc/ball clay body may be quite suitable as slowly fired whiteware, the accelerated heating/cooling shock to which raku objects are subjected puts a lot of demands on the clay body, and under these circumstances, the talc content may be working against you. In the article "A Potter's Notes on Thermal Expansion" (*Ceramics Monthly*, March 1979), Peter Sohngen notes that, "Lots of raku potters seem to be using talc, and getting away with it, but at raku temperatures it has exactly the opposite effect from what you want. In earthenware and whiteware (up to stoneware temperatures) talc in combination with clay produces enstatite, a mineral with high thermal expansion. [Talc appears in nonraku, low-fire bodies to help] prevent crazing, which may be a problem at low temperatures. Since at these temperatures talc makes the ware tighter and stronger, it is the most commonly used nonclay mineral in low-fire bodies." Additionally, in *The Potter's Dictionary of Materials and Techniques,* Frank Hamer observes that at bisque temperatures the magnesia in talc acts as a catalyst to convert free silica from quartz to cristobalite, which has a high coefficient of expansion.

To counter the thermal stress of the raku process, the best approach is to formulate a body from materials with as low thermal expansion as possible, then add further heat shock resistance in the form of sand, grog or other temper. Try using clays with low silica content, and grog instead of silica sand. The needlelike structure of F-1 wollastonite ($CaO \cdot SiO_2$) can lend plastic strength, and it also seems to improve resistance to cracking from heat stress. Coarsely ground raw kyanite ($Al_2O_3 \cdot SiO_2$) is a good addition because it will open the body like fine grog but has a much lower thermal expansion. As a starting point, you might wish to try the raku clay suggested in Peter Sohngen's article:

Raku Clay Body

A.P. Green Fireclay	90 parts
Tennessee Ball Clay (SGP 1)	15
Wollastonite (F-1)	5
Grog	7
Kyanite (35 mesh)	15
	132 parts

Spalling

I am having problems with a terra-cotta clay body which fires to Cone 4. My ware looks fine when removed from the kiln after bisquing, but begins to disintegrate after sitting in my kiln room for two or three weeks. Can you suggest a reason for my problem, and a solution?

Your clay body is probably spalling (chipping or fragmenting of clay, brick, stone, glass, concrete, etc.). The problem of spalling begins when lime particles enter the clay body through contaminated sand, clay or water. The original source of the lime may be in your studio where chips of plaster accidentally find their way into the clay, or there can be a contamination of the raw materials as they are manufactured. Contaminated sand is the most usual source of lime originating at manufacturing. During the bisque firing, lime dehydrates in the clay body. Being in a "thirsty" state, the lime begins to absorb water from the atmosphere and the ware. (Thus atmospheric humidity, clay porosity and absorption determine the length of time it takes for spalling to show up in the body—sometimes a matter of months.)

To help solve your spalling problem, first find out if there are lime particles in your fired ware. If you see a white speck near the center of each spalled surface, probe it with a needle tool or straight pin. If it crumbles easily, there is a good chance that it is lime. If you have leftover sand, clay and a water sample, drop a portion of each into beakers containing a 50% solution of hydrochloric acid. If bubbling takes place there is lime present.

I have been processing a local clay, but unfortunately some batches contain lime, which spalls after firing. Would it help to ball mill the clay, or is there some other solution?

Unless there is an overriding need for this specific clay, the best suggestion would be to avoid its use and look for deposits without lime contamination. Ball milling of large quantities of ingredients is not normally considered to be worthwhile with the potter's scale of equipment but the clay may, on an experimental basis, be reduced to slip so that larger particles settle out of the batch. Screening (40 mesh or smaller) can also be employed.

Warping

We have been doing some mural projects with a children's group, and have experienced some warping with the individual flat slabs that make up the murals. The warping appears before the pieces are fired. While the warping isn't objectionable in itself, it has presented some difficulties in adhering the fired clay slabs to the walls. Can you give us any hints on how we may avoid the warping? The clay we are using is a red-firing local clay; we are carving, painting and glazing the surfaces.

In general, flat slabs have a tendency to warp as they dry. There are several things you can do to minimize or eliminate this: 1) Grooves may be cut into the back side of the slab. Notice how this is done on commercial tiles. 2) Dry the slabs slowly, preferably between flat plaster bats that will absorb moisture from the clay. 3) If you don't have access to plaster bats, turn the clay slabs occasionally during the drying in order to help prevent warping. If the slabs are placed on layers of newspapers, the paper will absorb moisture from the clay.

I have some difficulty with warping of my thin, flat tiles, especially when coats of underglaze are applied. Can you tell me why?

The wetting of only one side of the tile or plate can cause warpage by creating a strain in the piece as it dries. You might try brushing the back of the piece with clear water after you've applied underglaze to the front—but don't use too much water. An equal wetting of the piece should help hold down warpage.

I have trouble firing wide, flaring bowl shapes in my electric kiln. This trouble is less pronounced in the bowls made with thick walls, but the very thin ones invariably warp. What causes this?

It is best to place thin, low, wide bowls in the center of the shelf, away from the elements, and stack the outer edges of the shelf with vertical shapes. The thinner the wall of the piece, the more important it is that the bowl receive even heat during the firing. If you are firing directly on the shelf, make sure there are no rough spots that might prevent even shrinkage of the foot of the bowl as it fires. Some potters spread a very thin coating of pure white sand on the shelf before firing delicate shapes; the grains of sand act like little roller bearings. Finally, fire more slowly when you have stacked the wide-mouthed shapes, particularly during the early part of the firing. You can slow down the firing while you're still on only one switch by leaving the peephole open and leaving the door ajar for an hour or two before closing the kiln completely.

GLAZES

GENERAL INFORMATION

What glaze ingredients require immediate use and prohibit storage in the wet state?

There are few materials that necessitate immediate use of the wet glaze batch, although some ingredients make use difficult without suitable adjustments. The only truly difficult glaze materials are those in the self-hardening category (plaster or portland cement, for example), and their addition to a glaze recipe is generally rare.

There are other glaze compounds which create problems, but which do not prohibit storage. Among these are colemanite and Gerstley borate, which have a tendency to flocculate (thicken) on standing. The flocculation tendency can be balanced by the addition of soda ash, sodium silicate or other deflocculant. But rather than adding deflocculants, many potters mix small batches and immediately use the recipes before flocculation becomes significant. Certain surface clays containing iron or alkaline compounds cannot be deflocculated. Should the Gerstley borate or colemanite glaze contain these, another factor is introduced which may prohibit successful deflocculation. Glazes which contain organic gum, binders or plasticizers tend to grow mold when stored too long, but substitutes are available which will not mold. Sometimes heavy substances like flint will settle to the bottom of the glaze container, and may be quite difficult to get back into suspension, but this can be achieved with sufficient mixing. Additions of 2% bentonite will help keep glaze particles in suspension and prevent settling. Occasionally some compounds will tend to form crystals in the glaze batch if it remains undisturbed. While this will alter the contents of the recipe slightly, it is usually not noticeable in the fired glaze; but crystals should be strained from the batch before use. (Regrind or heat in a little water to dissolve them and add back.)

Glazes containing soluble compounds (borax, for example) are sometimes confused with those creating storage problems. The symptoms are the same—the batch becomes unreliable with use, but usually the problem is that the glaze is poorly mixed. In that case, flux is removed with the water of each glaze application, but the other glaze materials remain with the batch in increasing proportions.

What is meant when glazes are referred to as lead, alkaline or fritted glazes? I have seen these words used by authors but have no clear idea of what they mean.

These classifications refer to the fluxing materials used in glazes to make the ingredients melt and fuse together. Lead, alkalines or frits usually are used for low-fire glazes. At the higher temperatures, feldspars generally are used and we speak of these as feldspathic glazes.

The unity formula is useful in analyzing and comparing glazes, listing the relationship between flux (RO), alumina (R_2O_3) and silica (RO_2). However, I have always questioned why boric oxide, a really active flux, is classed with alumina in the neutral column.

You are correct that boric oxide usually acts as a flux in glazes, but this compound also has qualities which fit in with both acid and neutral classifications. When boric oxide is shown in the (R_2O_3) neutral column, its chemical composition (B_2O_3) is the determining factor. Yet boric oxide is also considered acidic, and may appear along with the glass former, silica. Boric oxide is a good illustration that the unity formula is an abstraction—simply a way to think about materials classification—rather than an absolute. There are other compounds which appear to fit the system even more poorly than boric oxide, like phosphorus pentoxide (P_2O_5).

GLAZE MATERIALS

Materials and Their Effects

An old book of glaze recipes calls for siderite, pyrolusite, cassiterite and spartalite. Can you tell me if these materials are still available?

Major ceramics suppliers should have all the materials mentioned, but ceramists rarely use these mineral names today. Siderite is ferrous carbonate, pyrolusite is manganese dioxide, cassiterite is tin (stannic) oxide and spartalite is zinc oxide.

I want to try formulating an antique glaze which contains a substance called witherite. Could you tell me where this material is available or suggest a substitution?

Witherite is the relatively pure mineral form of barium carbonate, and the latter may be used as a direct substitute.

Since barium carbonate is toxic, couldn't barium oxide be substituted as a glaze ingredient? I believe this compound is used in hospitals for X-ray examinations.

Both barium carbonate and barium oxide are potentially toxic because of their solubility in weak acids. It is barium sulfate which is used for X-ray procedures.

What does lithium carbonate do in a glaze? Are there any substitutes if you run out of it?

Lithium carbonate is a strong alkaline compound with chemical qualities similar to high-temperature fluxes such as potassium or sodium. Because of its small atomic weight, you need not use as much lithium carbonate for an equal effect, though lithium compounds should increase glaze hardness and decrease expansion. A good substitute is spodumene, but it will require a minor adjustment in the glaze formula since it contains alumina and silica in addition to lithium.

Which of the potter's usual materials is most effective in the reduction of thermal expansion of clay and glazes?

39

Petalite generally tends to reduce thermal expansion to the greatest degree.

At a recent workshop, Oregon potter Tom Coleman mentioned amorphous silica as being more beneficial to the production of certain glazes than potter's flint. Can you tell me more about amorphous silica? Can I substitute it directly for flint in my glazes?

Amorphous silica is mined from extremely pure (99.5% SiO_2) sandstone deposits found mainly in Illinois and Missouri. Because of its cryptocrystalline structure (crystals too fine to be discerned readily under a microscope) and fine particle size (grade A-108 is 99% particles less than 8 microns), the prime uses of amorphous silica are as a filler in paints and as the main component in nonabrasive cleansers. Fine particle size could prove to be an advantage in glazes, too, since they tend to melt more readily; because of this, it may be advisable to substitute a smaller amount of amorphous silica for flint in most recipes to avoid excessive melting. However, amorphous silica, on firing, has more cristobalite development than potter's flint, and thus would render bodies less resistant to thermal shock.

Potter's flint, by the way, is not true flint, which is a black or brown cryptocrystalline quartz (the dark color is probably derived from carbonaceous material). In the United States, potter's flint is prepared by grinding a coarse crystalline, or macrocrystalline quartz, most commonly available at 200- and 325-mesh grades. The major supplier/producer of amorphous silica (at the time of this writing) is Illinois Minerals Company, 2035 Washington Avenue, Cairo, Illinois 62914.

Because of its very fine particle size, amorphous silica poses additional inhalation risks to the potter. Discuss this with supplier before using this product.

A number of glazes I wish to try call for the chemical sodium silico fluoride. I cannot find this compound in the West—it isn't even mentioned in any of my books. Would you tell me what it is, where I can buy it, or what I might substitute?

Sodium silico fluoride will introduce two strong fluxes with silica into the glaze without the presence of alumina. Commonly used as a medium- to high-fire flux, this compound is also known as sodium fluosilicate. A strong modifier of color, it may also produce cratered surfaces because of the volatile nature of fluorine, a substantial part of its formula (Na_2SiF_6). Sodium silico fluoride is obtainable at a few of the larger ceramics suppliers, and also through chemical supply houses found in major cities. Its additional uses as a "laundry sour" and as an insecticide suggest other properties of the compound and additional sources of supply.

Glaze calculation will allow the substitution of a variety of fluorine compounds for sodium silico fluoride, including fluorspar (CaF_2); and where alumina is desired, cryolite (Na_3AlF_6)—also known as sodium fluoaluminate. Sodium silico fluoride, however, should not be confused with the poisonous crystalline salts sodium fluoride (NaF) and sodium bifluoride ($NaHF_2$). Adequate kiln ventilation is very important when firing fluoride compounds.

I am interested in the oxides of molybdenum and am wondering if you could tell me how this metal is used in ceramic glazes.

The oxides of molybdenum serve two principal purposes in glazes: first, they tend to produce a cloudy blue color, and second, molybdenum greatly reduces the viscosity of glazes when introduced in amounts as small as 0.1%, particularly in the high-fire range. This metallic element is said to resemble chromium and tungsten in many of its properties. Of all the chemical elements, molybdenum is by itself quite refractory, possessing one of the highest melting points (2620°C). When combined in glazes, however (principally as molybdenum trioxide), this melting point is substantially reduced. If somewhat erratic results are noted in glazes containing molybdenum, it may be because of the slight solubility of the trioxide form.

Molybdenum trioxide should be handled with caution because of its potential toxicity. Avoid breathing or ingesting the compound.

My experimentation has been confined to ash glazes, basically using a formula of:

Ash Glaze

(Cone 9–10)

Plastic Vitrox	50–90 %
Various Ashes	10–50
Clay	0–35

I have obtained excellent results with this recipe fired in a gas kiln but now have been informed by my supplier that his source of plastic vitrox has ceased production. What can I substitute to produce the same results?

Plastic vitrox, a feldspathic clay mined in California, continues to be available on a limited basis. Used as a high silica source of potassium and alumina in clays and glazes, the mineral can produce a porcelain-like body when finely ground. One analysis is: CaO–0.22, K_2O–6.81, MgO–0.20, Na_2O–0.29, Al_2O_3–14.87, Fe_2O_3–0.09, SiO_2–75.56, loss on ignition–2.04, and shrinkage–15.4% at Cone 10. If plastic vitrox remains unavailable through your usual sources, one supplier recommends a direct substitution of:

Plastic Vitrox Substitute

Kingman Feldspar	45 %
Edgar Plastic Kaolin	17
Flint (325 mesh)	38
	100 %

Many glaze formulas that I use have clay as a basic part of the formula. Which kind of clay should I use?

The type of clay used in a glaze can affect the results obtained, so specific clays should be identified in each formula. When the kind of clay is not shown in the recipe, the most frequently used clays are good substitutions. Kaolin is probably the most frequently used clay in glaze formulation. One reason for its broad use is that it is virtually free of impurities such as iron or manganese, and so does not add any color of its own to the glaze. Ball clay is also used frequently in glazes, but it is much more plastic than kaolin and also has a few impurities which give it a gray color when fired.

We live near a large stream which is littered with smooth granite stones ranging in size from 3 to 10 inches in diameter. I have often thought about making glaze from such rock but it would take forever to break it up. I am aware that jaw crushers and hammermills are available for potters, but heavy machinery is not my style. Is there any simple way I can turn a little granite into a little glaze?

Hammermills and crushers have their place in the potter's repertoire of equipment, as do slab rollers and potter's wheels, but are not required for turning rock into glaze. Your kiln is an excellent processing tool: granite can simply be bisque fired, rendering it so completely fractured that the rocks can even be broken up with the hands. A small sledgehammer will further break down the now soft rock enough to sufficiently screen it to the desired mesh (generally from 60 to 200); the smaller the particle size, the lower the temperature at which the batch will melt.

Rocks do not tend to blow up in the kiln, as is widely believed, except when they contain enough water to produce steam. The same is true for a pot. If the rocks are sufficiently dry and the potter avoids overloading the kiln floor, this should be enough precaution. Ceramists who live in regions where rocks might contain quantitites of boron or lead may wish to test small samples before firing large batches; such materials may flux significantly even in a bisque firing. In most regions worldwide, this is not a concern.

Feldspars

A glaze recipe calls for orthoclase feldspar but this material is not listed by my supplier. Is there a substitute?

Orthoclase feldspar is the mineral name for potash feldspar. Custer is one common brand available from suppliers nationally.

After ordering Cornwall stone for making a porcelain glaze, the supplier sent Cornish stone instead. I read that both are the same thing, but when substituted, the raw Cornish stone glaze was unexpectedly greenish and of a completely different texture. Did I get the wrong material, or would grinding to reduce the particle size help?

Cornish stone, Cornwall stone, China stone and pegmatite are synonyms for the same material. But it is available in two grades—raw stone, which contains fluorine; and defluorinated, which is purer. There are also "hard" and "soft" varieties—referring to fusibility—that might affect the glaze texture. The green tint you experienced could be a combination of fluorine with other glaze ingredients. Grinding or milling the Cornish stone will not change the fluorine coloration, but might improve the glaze texture.

Several of my glaze recipes contain Buckingham feldspar which is not available from my supplier. Is there a material which will substitute?

Custer feldspar is very similar, and in most glazes it may be directly substituted for Buckingham.

I have determined that a glaze problem is the result of the changed character of a specific feldspar which for years I have purchased from the same supplier. Is there anything the potter can do about the unreliability of feldspar composition?

"Most studio potters are buying (feldspar) by brand name which, over a period of time, can get them in big trouble," states Hammill & Gillespie, Inc., importers and manufacturers of nonmetallic mineral products and chemicals. Potters, they continue, "need an appreciable amount of consumer education, particularly to understand that the formula of five years ago may not work using current production of a particular brand of feldspar. They also need to know how to compute molecular formulae so that they can see what effect a change in the feldspar they use may have on their ware.

"We (Hammill & Gillespie) can supply to interested customers an analysis of each lot of feldspar they buy. If they would...request this of their suppliers, they would be better informed, provided they understand which variations are significant and which are of slight consequence."

In reading glaze recipes in *Ceramics Monthly* and in my ceramics library, I am appalled by the great number of feldspars that it must be necessary to keep in stock for

glaze making. Are all of these necessary or can feldspars be substituted for one another?

Two or three feldspars should enable you to get a good range of glazes. If you have a potash feldspar, a soda feldspar and nepheline syenite, you should be able to substitute one of these for almost any feldspar called for in a recipe. It may be necessary to run tests to find the correct substitution, and perhaps even make some adjustments in the other materials.

Lead Compounds

On a trip through Europe recently I visited the studios of several folk potters and was surprised to find that some of them were using a yellow form of lead for their glaze work. I have been familiar only with white lead and would like to know what this yellow lead is.

The yellow form of lead is called "litharge" or lead sulfide. Like other forms of raw lead, it is not used much in the U.S. among studio potters because of the obvious lead hazard. Litharge sometimes contains impurities and has a larger particle size than white lead.

Since becoming interested in wall tiles, I have tested many glazes in the Cone 06–04 range. The ones containing fritted or unfritted lead are generally the simplest, most pleasing and dependable. The dangers of lead in the studio are well known, so I feel a bit apprehensive about using this flux on a regular basis. Are my fears justified, or can precautions make lead a viable glaze ingredient?

One of the foremost glaze experts once commented that if he had the power to lock up lead around the world in the safest possible conditions, he would fuse this potentially toxic material in glaze. The key to lead safety from the product usage standpoint is that the glaze be properly formulated, that is, solidly bonded to alumina and silica molecules so that it is no longer soluble (toxic). In the case of wall tiles, lead release is not the problem that it is with dinnerware—wall tiles will not be coming into contact with foods to be ingested. Thus glazes which fit properly and which are structurally sound will be quite adequate for this usage. The problem in making wall tiles is with the potter's exposure during production. Lead compounds should be handled in the strictest conditions of studio hygiene. Use of a low-solubility lead frit is recommended over other alternatives. Ceramists who work continually with lead would be wise to consult their personal physician regarding the advisability and frequency of testing for lead poisoning. Lead can be used and handled in the studio with knowledge and meticulous hygiene, without adverse effect on the ceramist. It can be formulated in glazes with extremely low lead release that are safe in all manner of applications for the user. But if you feel inadequately prepared to manage technical matters in the case of lead, then using commercial glazes might be a good introduction to materials management. While many of these premixed recipes also contain lead, the potter's responsibility excludes formulation but still includes good studio hygiene, thorough mixing before use and firing exactly as directed. Or, if you simply don't feel good about handling toxic materials, then consider switching into mid-range or high-fire ceramics where lead is not as essential for first quality, consistent glaze surfaces.

Boron Compounds

Could you please tell me a little about Gerstley borate?

Gerstley borate is a relatively impure form of colemanite, a mixture of colemanite and ulexite with quantities of magnesia, carbon dioxide, clay and water included in its composition. It is an inexpensive source of boric oxide as well as calcium in glazes, and proves an excellent flux for controlling the maturing point of glazes.

Some of my glaze recipes call for calcined borax, but I can't find it listed in ceramics supply catalogs. I tried to calcine raw borax in a Cone 06 firing, but got glass. Can you tell me at what temperature borax can be calcined?

Water may be expelled from raw borax by heating it to Cone 016. This material, known as anhydrous or fused borax, will be in a glassy state, but should be soft enough to dry grind by hand or in a ball mill. Calcined borax may be stored in an air-tight glass container, or quickly weighed and used before it can reabsorb water from the atmosphere. It is often advantageous to substitute raw borax for calcined borax and thus avoid calcining and dry storage altogether. In that case, for every part of anhydrous borax, use 1.89 parts of the hydrated (raw) material. Fused borax sold commercially may resemble a powder but is actually composed of small glassy pellets. Anhydrous borax is not a common item at most ceramics suppliers, but is available from chemical supply houses catering to laboratories or school chemistry departments.

Many potters who live outside of the United States are unable to obtain certain materials used in glazes included in *Ceramics Monthly* articles, either because of the prohibitive cost of shipping or because some glaze ingredients simply aren't available. One of the common problem ingredients is colemanite. Can you give a substitute for this compound?

In a past issue of *Ceramic Review* magazine, ceramist Edwin Todd gave the following recipe:

Colemanite Substitute

Boric Acid	58.43 %
Magnesite	3.13
Strontium Carbonate	0.37
Whiting	33.32
Cullet	0.17
Flint	4.58
	100.00 %

He further commented, "Boric acid causes us no trouble as we keep our glazes dry and only mix what we will use at one time." Potters wishing to use this substitute should be aware that magnesite is generally sold as magnesium carbonate.

Frits

Many of the glazes published in *Ceramics Monthly* list frits as part of the recipe. What is a frit and why is it used?

A frit is a batch of materials that has been melted

into a glass, then pulverized again for use in a glaze. This may be done to render soluble materials insoluble and thus prevent the loss of any ingredients by being absorbed into the body. It may be done to change a toxic material to a harmless form. It also may be done to expel gases and thus eliminate the chance of blisters or bubbles in the glaze. Finally, the frit may be used to lower the melting point of a glaze.

Can you suggest a frit to replace borax in a glaze? My current recipe is 50% borax and 50% Gerstley borate for raku firing.

There are a number of good frit substitutions for borax in a glaze, and these can be directly substituted and tried experimentally in raku glazes, although in other recipes they require some recalculation. Try Ferro Frit 3185 (contains sodium, too), Hommel Frit K-3 (sodium and calcium added), Hommel 385 (with barium), Pemco Frit P-54 (with sodium and calcium), Pemco Frit P-318 (with barium), Pemco Frit P-830 (with sodium and calcium) Pemco Frit P-1413 (with calcium). Use these frits with additions of from 20 to 60% clay on an experimental basis. For specifics on these frit compositions, see "Frit Formulas" in the May 1978 *Ceramics Monthly.*

Your glaze of 50% borax and 50% Gerstley borate, however, is extremely unstable, very susceptible to acid attack and cannot be recommended for functional ware without additions of clay for durability.

Is there an alternative to using toxic barium carbonate? The sulfate does not perform well in my glazes.

Industry has long recognized the need for a safer form of barium, and in instances where the potter's exposure might be excessive, specially formulated frits are substituted. At least two of the major manufacturers formulate barium frits to include only barium, alumina and silica—rendering the barium insoluble. These alternatives to the use of barium carbonate sometimes require reformulation of the glaze batch recipe, and are sold under the brand names of Ferro Frit 3247, and Pemco Frit P-318. Consult your local ceramics supplier for further information.

Leafing through some back issues of *Ceramics Monthly*, I noticed that glaze articles many times included the use of Hommel Frit 14. Could you give its empirical formula?

Hommel Frit 14 has the following empirical formula: Na_2O–0.32, CaO–0.68, B_2O_3–0.64, SiO_2–1.47. Since it contains no lead, this frit is useful for fluxing low-temperature glazes that might come in contact with foods.

I have been switching from lead-fluxed glazes, but find that low-fire glaze formulation with a boron frit (Ferro 3229) is not as easily achieved as with lead. It appears that the batch must be more exact, and the firing range is shorter. Is there any reason for these differences?

The low-fire boron glaze characteristically melts quicky over a short temperature range, and thus is much more sensitive to errors in batch content. During the firing cycle, lead glazes are glassy longer than their boron counterparts and thus are less apt to show defects from under- or overfiring. However, the insoluble frit is the least problematic source of boron. With reasonable care in formulation of the batch, consistent firing practices, and a short "soak" at the end of the firing, high-quality boron glazes can be repeatedly produced.

Opacifiers

I have some Ultrox, a glaze chemical I believe is an opacifier, but am not really sure. Can you tell me its use, and how it is calculated into a glaze formula? Do you know what percentages should be used in an average glaze, and if it has any additional effects?

Ultrox is a trade name for a group of opacifiers which can be calculated in the glaze formula as zirconium silicate (ZrO_2SiO_2). Ultrox Standard is perhaps the most common form purchased by potters. When used as an opacifier in white or pastel glazes, the amount added to the glaze generally ranges from 15–18%. Since the average particle size of an opacifier greatly affects its performance (smaller particles yield more opacifying strength), three other particle sizes are offered under the Ultrox name—

Ultrox 500W, 1000W and 2000W. The strongest of these (2000W) has an average particle size of ½ micron, while Ultrox Standard is rated at an average particle size of two microns. These opacifiers will also decrease the thermal expansion of a glaze formula and so will reduce crazing.

I have just set up a studio and am trying to formulate some opaque recipes. Several previously used formulas call for tin oxide, but with my present budget I find the cost prohibitive. Could Zircopax or Opax be substituted for the tin? How much should be used? How do the compositions of these opacifiers compare?

You can make the substitutions mentioned, but there will probably be some differences, such as a loss of some of the smoothness of the glaze surface and a decrease in brilliance of the white obtained. A suggested starting point for substitution would be to use twice as much Zircopax or Opax.

Zircopax contains tin oxide (0.22%) and zirconium oxide, while Opax contains no tin oxide and a stronger concentration of zirconium oxide (90.84% compared to 64.88% for Zircopax). Opax also contains some sodium which is not present in Zircopax.

You might be surprised to know that our largest supplier in the area does not handle calcined zinc oxide which seems to be more foolproof than the standard product. How high would I have to fire it to get the water out?

You can calcine almost any ceramic material by taking it just to red heat (about 1500°F) to remove chemically combined water.

Soluble Compounds

How does one store potassium carbonate (also called pearl ash) to keep it from sweating or picking up moisture from damp air? I have tried storing it in plastic bags, and even inside other containers, but it still eats through to affect the paint on my shelves. I am now using glass jars, but if they are left open or only loosely fastened, the compound collects moisture. If I close them tightly, the water inside cannot escape and droplets appear on the jar

even though the chemical seems dry when sealed. Is there an effective way to store this compound, or should I substitute another glaze material?

The problem is not with the damp air, but rather with the glaze ingredient. Potassium carbonate (K_2CO_3) is deliquescent, which makes it difficult to handle, since the term applies to materials which naturally tend to pull water from the surrounding air, and which tend to remain in the hydrated state. This may be a problem when attempting to accurately weigh the ingredient, since pearl ash will be in weaker concentration when wet than when in the dry state.

Potassium carbonate is also soluble, which tends to make it unsuitable for glaze use except when fritted, since the fluxing power follows the water rather than the glaze solids. Unreliable effects are the result. Finally, pearl ash is rather caustic.

Thus, substitution is usually a good idea. Frits with a high potassium content are one choice, and Ferro 3819 (Pemco P-25 or Hommel 259) might be a good substitute on an experimental basis.

If pearl ash is required for suitable results in a specific recipe, the only really acceptable storage method is in tightly sealed glass containers. Contrary to their appearance, plastic jars and bottles may be slightly porous, and thus unsuitable for storing this unusual glaze material.

I have a bottle of Epsom salts (the kind found in the medicine chest) and have been told that this material is useful in glazes. If this is true, can you tell me what Epsom salts is, and how it functions in the glaze recipe?

Epsom salts is hydrated magnesium sulfate ($MgSO_4 \cdot 7H_2O$, also known as magnesium sulfate heptahydrate). This material is usually added in small quantities to glaze as a flocculant (0.3 grams Epsom salts to 100 grams of glaze), thickening the batch without reducing its water content. In larger quantities, Epsom salts may also act as a flux in the stoneware firing range. In that case, effects produced are similar to magnesium carbonate or dolomite; but the solubility of Epsom salts can cause erratic results when used in significant quantities.

Glaze Binders

Do you have any information on the dry strength of gum tragacanth compared to gum arabic?

Gum tragacanth exhibits more than twice the dry strength of gum arabic, although some of the cellulose derivatives, such as Union Carbide Corporation's hydroxy ethyl cellulose, exhibit nearly 50% more dry strength than gum tragacanth.

We live in the country and have little access to ceramics supplies, except by mail order. Our objective is to eventually use only materials which are available locally. Up until now we have been using a commercial binder to minimize chipping of unfired glaze surfaces during decorating and handling. Is there any easily obtained general-purpose product which can be substituted for commercial binder, and what would be good ratio of binder to dry glaze?

Karo syrup has been used by many potters as a good quality substitute for commercial binder. Its only drawback is a tendency to encourage the growth of mold in glazes, but this can be overcome by adding syrup only to that portion of the batch used. One teaspoon of syrup for each 100 grams of dry glaze is a standard addition. While binders will tend to cut handling losses in large-scale commercial potteries and are useful for certain specialized glazing techniques, the material is generally an unnecessary glaze constituent, particularly in recipes with high clay content.

Can you tell me how to prepare CMC (carboxy methel cellulose) gum to use as a binder in a glaze? I am sure that I didn't prepare it properly for I found that it was almost impossible to put through an 80-mesh screen. In another batch, using more water than suggested, I had trouble making the glaze adhere to the bisque.

Put one ounce of the dry powder into a quart jar and add a cup of hot water. Stir this and let it stand for a few hours. Then add another cup of hot water, stir very thoroughly, and let this stand overnight. Fill the jar with water, shake the mixture well, and it is ready for use. Sometimes it is necessary to dilute this mixture even more with water. Since CMC is synthetic, it is not as likely to sour as are the organic binders, gum arabic and gum tragacanth.

COLOR AND TEXTURE

Colorants

Besides being a potter, I am a lapidary, and it occurred to me recently, after grinding and polishing lapis lazuli stones and cleaning silicon carbide and mineral sludge from the settling tank, that I could use this waste material in glazes. What is your opinion?

Lapis lazuli is mainly composed of lazurite, but also hauynite, iron pyrite and sodalite. This azure blue mineral in powdered form has historically been an artist's pigment, producing ultra-marine blue. The potter inclined to experimentation could dry the ground residue and add it to glaze or overglaze as a colorant percentage. Silicon carbide from the grinding wheel may cause boiling and/or local reduction and the sodium content could somewhat increase glaze flow. Sulfur and chlorine in lapis lazuli call for good ventilation around the kiln.

Since grindings are a waste product in lapidary work, many ground, mixed minerals may be found in the workshops of stonecutters or from rock shops. Calcining these materials by firing them to bisque temperature in a crucible is a good first step in their successful use.

Can you tell me the composition of yellow ocher? Can I use it as a high-temperature yellow colorant to substitute for a commercial vanadium stain?

Yellow ocher is hydrated ferric (iron) oxide, and its formula is generally shown as $Fe_2O_3 \cdot H_2O$; it may contain some clay and other impurities. This compound is quite a different material than vanadium stain. However, when mixed with zinc oxide and rutile, it has been reported that yellow ocher will produce a high-temperature yellow, though not as strong as vanadium stain.

Is manganese particularly difficult to use as a colorant? I have been trying to get some brownish-purple glazes with it, but seem to get a blistered surface instead of a smooth glaze. The color is right but the texture certainly isn't.

It sounds as if you either are using too much colorant or are underfiring. Try refiring one of the pieces to see if the glaze smooths out. If you don't get better results, try cutting down on the amount of manganese you are using. Manganese dioxide generally is used at about a 2% addition.

If a recipe states that rutile is to be used, does it mean granular or powdered?

Powdered rutile is intended unless otherwise noted.

Due to the cost of cobalt, are there substitutes to obtain medium and dark blues?

Blue colors in ceramics are produced primarily by cobalt, but also by copper, iron, nickel and zirconium. There is really no substitute for cobalt because it gives a consistent, strong blue throughout the potter's firing range. The closest colorant is Harshaw's periwinkle blue stain which is very stable and consistent to Cone 5.

But there are a few tricks to buying and using cobalt that might help you obtain an economical application of the material. If you are a high-firing potter, use cobalt in glazes containing potash feldspar (instead of soda feldpar, as the color tends to be more brilliant, requiring less cobalt content). Low-fire glazes typically have good cobalt blue brilliancy. When buying cobalt, ask your supplier for the percentage analysis of the ground ore. Ceramic grade is generally from 70 to 71% Co_2O_3, but there are other grades including a metallurgical one as high as 76%. Some simple glaze calculation can also help you determine whether a unit of cobalt is currently less expensive in the carbonate or oxide form from your supplier.

Does copper or chromium make a stronger green for use as an underglaze?

There are major advantages in using chromium as a source of green in underglazes because of its strength, opacity and inability to become part of the formation of glaze. Copper, on the other hand, is easily diffused and highly soluble in the glaze, rendering its color transparent, except in very large quantities. Barium, calcium and magnesium compounds increase the clarity of chrome greens, while calcium fluoride in conjunction with chromium produces an especially handsome, rich shade.

I am working with a Cone 6 matt glaze from the *Ceramics Monthly* handbook, *Glaze Projects*, and find this to be an excellent recipe for oxidation firing. However, in experimenting with colorants I found that chrome oxide gives unsatisfactory results—the surface is excessively dry. Can you explain this?

The behavior of chrome is an exception to the usual effects of coloring oxides in that it acts very much like alumina in a glaze, tending to increase the maturing point. In small quantities (0.1–1%), however, this colorant may serve quite well.

I occasionally see reference to pink and lavender colors made with cobalt, and wonder if you can tell me the conditions under which these colors are obtained?

Cobalt is used in combination with boron, magnesium and silica in order to produce pinks and lavenders. A very small amount of cobalt is used in order to avoid a strong blue that might dominate the color.

I have been using a very fine base glaze, but wish to achieve a consistent tint that eliminates the speckling which occurs when cobalt oxide is added as a colorant. Is there a way to do this without using a ball mill or other grinding equipment?

Cobalt carbonate will disperse more readily than the simple oxide, and is a good substitution.

In "Do-It-Yourself Glaze Stains," an article published in the May 1960 *Ceramics Monthly*, Karl Martz gave the following advice: "To achieve a delicate blue without specks, add a few drops of a strong cobalt sulfate solution to the glaze slip. Go easy, however, because more than a few drops of such an acid solution will cause the glaze slip to flocculate or gel into a pasty mass which is very difficult to apply. To avoid this difficulty, neutralize the sulfate with soda ash."

I have been making terra-cotta platters decorated with various layers of slip colored with commercial stains. These are oxidation fired to Cone 04–03. Can you suggest a matt or semimatt gloss finish that would be just enough to give the color a little spark? The unglazed pieces seem dead; the clear-glazed ones are too shiny. I've been testing various semigloss combinations without notable success. Matt glazes I've tried tend to gray the following black slip which I would prefer remain black:

Gill's Black Slip (Cone 04–03)

Ball Clay	23.0 %
Cedar Heights Redart Clay	48.0
Black Iron Oxide	4.9
Black Stain (Mason)	10.6
Manganese Dioxide	13.5
	100.0 %

How can I get the results I'm after?

There are a variety of methods used to liven slip color without resorting to glossy surfaces: Prior to bisque firing or after bisque firing, the piece can be lightly sprayed with a shiny glaze—not enough to turn glossy, but just enough to "wet" the color. It takes very little spray to achieve this effect, which can be applied either with a spray gun or airbrush. After bisque firing slip-decorated ware, there are some other alternatives: A shiny glaze may be drastically thinned and the ware dipped in the batch; or the slip-decorated and bisqued ware can be dipped in a normal glaze batch which is then wiped away with a sponge. The residue is sufficient to wet the colors.

In most reduction glazes, iron produces green or celadon, but in some cases it makes an earthy cream/tan/yellow. What is the difference? How can I predict which base glazes will produce what colors? I am looking for a Cone 6 reduction glaze that would give me a creamy yellow, iron-spotted matt—preferably without barium. What's the answer?

Most iron glazes which produce the classic celadon green in reduction will produce a tan or cream or yellow when fired in oxidation or in a neutral atmosphere. Most potters are unhappy with such results when seeking green instead, but your creamy yellow results are much easier to obtain. If iron spotting in oxidation is insufficient, try adding granular manganese as needed to achieve enough ironlike flecks. Since most classic celadons are not matts, increase the alumina content for a true matt glaze without underfiring, or select a magnesia base glaze, since these form good matts and discourage celadon greens at the same time.

Ceramic Stains

I have been producing porcelain ware glazed with recipes colored by ceramic stain additions to the same transparent base. Though I have heard that most of these stains are stable at high temperatures, I have been unable to obtain a decent deep pink or lavender at Cone 9. Could you suggest a reliable stain, or tell me some way to get the colors I want?

Most likely your difficulty lies in the ingredients in your base glaze or in your firing procedure, since stain manufacturers indicate their colors are stable to Cone 12. In a recent discussion with a representative of Mason Color and Chemical Works, East Liverpool, Ohio, suggestions were offered for obtaining the maximum color results from ceramic stains in glazes: Calcium enhances most colors (with the exception of browns) and should be used as the major flux, with perhaps 12–15% whiting in the base. If the base has a high content of boron (Gerstley borate, colemanite, a boron frit) or alkalies (soda and potash beyond the quantities typically found in feldspars), it may act as a solvent on the stain during melting, thus destroying the tint.

Of the available pink stains, chrome-tin mixtures provide the deepest colors and the shades closest to red at higher temperatures. There are other pink stains, such as chrome-alumina and manganese-alumina, but these are more pastel. Chrome-tin pinks generally have more of a bluish cast, and together with cobalt blue stains are used to produce purples and violets. Beneficial to strengthening color are additions (to the base glaze) of calcium, tin; detrimental to pinks and lavenders from the chrome-tin combination are magnesium, zinc, phosphorus and antimony. Barium and lithium compounds seem to have no noticeable effect when present in small amounts. When boric oxide is present, the calcium oxide to boric oxide ratio should be kept 3:1. If the base glaze is low in calcium, an addition of whiting or wollastonite along with the stain is suggested. Alumina and silica in the base seems to be useful in reducing the solvent action of the glaze on the stain.

The following were suggested as bases suitable for producing colored glazes with stain additions:

Base Glaze I (Cone 4–5)

Lead Carbonate	12.41 %
Whiting	21.17
Kona F-4 Feldspar	25.18
Kaolin	8.39
Flint	32.85
	100.00 %

The previous glaze contains lead in a toxic form and should only be used by ceramists familiar with safe handling, firing and testing procedures of lead compounds.

Base Glaze II (Cone 9)

Barium Carbonate	2.2 %
Whiting	15.7
Custer Feldspar	37.4
Edgar Plastic Kaolin	11.7
Flint	33.0
	100.0 %
Add: Zinc Oxide	6.8 %

Base Glaze II should work well with most brown stains, which require the presence of zinc for optimum color. For colors other than brown, try removing the zinc; an addition of small amounts (2–5%) whiting or wollastonite may be necessary for adjustment.

Base Glaze III (Cone 12–14)

Barium Carbonate ....0.28 %
Boric Acid 0.59
Magnesium Carbonate 0.59
Whiting 13.12
Frit 3467 (Ferro) 19.82
Custer Feldspar 20.38
Nepheline Syenite 9.21
Kaolin 8.37
Kentucky Ball Clay (5) 4.75
Flint..22.89
⠀⠀⠀⠀⠀⠀⠀⠀⠀⠀⠀⠀⠀⠀⠀⠀⠀⠀⠀⠀⠀100.00 %
Add: Any Stain ....10.00 %

This final glaze was developed by a Canadian company that produced ware with Victoria green and chrome-tin pink glazes at the temperatures indicated. The flint, frit and kaolin were ball milled with the color for 10 hours, then the balance of the materials was added and the batch was ground for an additional 24 hours. This recipe might offer a good starting point for those wishing to develop high-temperature pinks. Perhaps a few adjustments such as decreasing the flint, increasing whiting and feldspar, would lower the maturity to within the reach of most electric kilns, without greatly affecting color.

Victoria greens (a sodium or potassium dichromate, flint, calcium carbonate mixture) and chrome-tin pinks do tend to fade at about Cone 9, but maintaining an optimum oxidation atmosphere may slow this process. In gas kilns, the gas-air ratio should be 1:10; in electric kilns, try firing with a kiln ventilation system or with both bottom and top peephole plugs out.

Can you suggest a good proportion to mix vanadium and tin in order to calcine a stain for use at Cone 10? I have found my results currently produce a very watery pale color. Is tin the only additive commonly used in a vanadium stain?

Calcined tin oxide and vanadium pentoxide have been used alone as a ceramic stain, but do tend to produce a rather weak color. Because of this, small amounts of titanium dioxide are often added to intensify the yellow; or alumina is sometimes added to alter the hue. In preparation, extensive grinding should be avoided. Vanadium stain is best added to glazes which are low in alkaline content, since highly alkaline glazes tend to bleach the yellow. In addition, vanadium yellow tends to be an oxidation color and may turn gray to blue in reduction. Because of the general weakness of all vanadium stains, they are added in relatively large amounts as compared to other colorants—usually in a range from 5 to 10% of the batch glaze recipe.

I have been using tin-vanadium yellow stain with my glazes for a very long time with beautiful results. But this compound has become so expensive that it now costs almost five times as much as what I used to pay. Why can't I combine yellow stain with my own tin to produce a similar, less expensive result?

If the yellow stain you wish to substitute is in fact a vanadium yellow, you can add this to any tin glaze in your firing range, and the chances are quite good that you will get a fine, yellow result. Tin is used with vanadium in order to brighten an otherwise weak yellow color, and it need not be combined in the stain in order to have this effect. But there are less expensive yellow stains like Mason's 6485.

Copper Reds

Can I get copper red colors with mishima techniques?

Copper reds are possible and have been demonstrated by the Japanese potter Shin Fujihira using copper oxide and mishima methods. He uses an ash glaze over the copper slip applied to greenware. The glaze contains 30% wood ash, 40% feldspar and 30% rice straw ash. The firing is reduced, as is the custom with most copper reds.

Can you tell me if it is possible through multiple firings or whatever to achieve copper reds in crystalline glazes?

It is not uncommon to develop crystalline glazes which have a rose petal pink in oxidation using copper and a high titanium content in a traditional crystalline base glaze. Tests using local reduction materials in crystalline glazes demonstrate the conflict between the thinness of the crystalline glaze surface and the thickness required to achieve a suitable locally reduced copper red; thus, silicon carbide-produced copper reds appear as if the red effects have burned off.

But we have also heard reports of true copper red crystal glazes produced by first firing in the typical crystalline manner in oxidation, then lowering the temperature below that which the crystals are formed, and reducing.

Crackle Glazes

I am working with stoneware fired to Cone 6 and would like very much to find a crackle glaze formula. Can you provide one or tell me something about crackling in glaze and its effects on the clay body?

Crackling (also known as crazing) results from a variety of causes, including excessive thermal shock (too fast cooling in the kiln), the freezing and thawing of ware, and the action of moisture expanding porous bodies. But the most common cause of crazing is a poor fit between body and glaze where the shrinkage of the latter during the cooling cycle exceeds clay shrinkage, causing cracks in the glaze surface as the only means to relieve stresses between the two materials. Thus, crazing cannot be discussed only in terms of the glaze, but the thermal expansion of the body must also be taken into account. Nearly any glaze can be made to crackle if applied to a low-shrinkage body, or if sufficient silica is removed from the glaze or the body. Use of a finer mesh silica in glaze can cure crazing of some glazes (but finer silica can pose special problems of studio hygiene). One way to increase crazing (say, from a large-patterned system of cracks to a finely spaced crackle) is to increase high-shrinkage materials in the glaze, such as sodium, potassium and calcium.

Ware may emerge crazed from the kiln, or crazing may take place over a period of weeks to years as body and glaze adjust to strong or subtle differences in thermal expansion, respectively. If the glaze coating is under tension (resulting in crazing), body strength may be reduced by as much as 25% of the unglazed bisque. Conversely, glazes under compression increase body strength, though excessive compression leads to glaze failure in the form of shivering. The strongest situation for the body is for the glaze to be under mild compression, leaving room for the body to slightly expand (due to heat or moisture absorption) and the glaze to remain craze free.

Is it possible to get a crackle glaze at stoneware temperature? If so, would it be all right to use it on vases and other pieces that are supposed to hold water?

Stoneware glazes crackle on occasion but since stoneware clay is impervious to water there is no great harm in using glazes that crackle. For decorative objects, they are especially suitable. However, one difficulty may arise: the cracks in the glaze are so tight—that is, there is so little space in the cracks—that a ceramic stain or fine oil paint can't be rubbed in to bring out the pattern of the crackle. Only a dye will stain the cracks and this isn't satisfactory because it will fade in a short time.

But there is a liquid which will penetrate and give strong color to the cracks in a crackled piece of stoneware. Add 1 part sulfuric acid to 12 parts water and mix slowly and carefully in a plastic bowl. Dissolve sugar in this dilute acid until you have a saturated solution. Then soak the crackle-glazed pot in the liquid for a given time and check the time: depending on the pot, one or two minutes should be enough. If the pot is soaked too long, the color of the crackle will be too strong. On the other hand, if the pot is not immersed in the liquid long enough, there will be insufficient color.

Sponge off the liquid carefully and wipe the pot clean. Place it in your kitchen oven and heat it to 300°F for ten minutes or more. Keep looking into the oven and when the crackle becomes good and black, remove the finished pot.

In a 300° oven, the sugar and acid react, turning the sugar to carbon. Since the sugar and acid solution has been absorbed into even the finest cracks in the glaze, the crackle lines are blackened.

To get a blacker color, repeat the process of soaking and heating. If the color is too strong (from soaking too long in the liquid), heat the pot at 500° until all the color in the cracks disappears. Then resoak the pot for a shorter period of time.

Crystalline Glazes

All the crystal glazes I've seen are based on zinc. Are there other ceramic elements or compounds which form crystals?

You have probably seen a variety of crystalline glazes without actually thinking about it, as many glazes contain small crystals, although the effect is not so pronounced. But macrocrystals are commonly formed by iron, titanium and zinc. Less commonly known crystal producers are bismuth and manganese. Small amounts of lithium, molybdenum, tungsten and vanadium are sometimes added to glazes to promote seeding by these crystal producers.

Underglaze

Can you explain the difference between a slip, engobe and underglaze? These terms seem to be used rather loosely and I am confused about what they are and when to use a specific product.

Slips and engobes are the same. They contain a large amount of clay and a small amount of colorant. Underglazes are mostly colorant with just a small amount of clay added as a binder. The underglaze is more intense in color and more versatile to use. It can be used either on greenware or bisque; slips or engobes usually cannot be used on bisqueware without danger of peeling or flaking.

I have been experimenting with dry underglaze powders sold by some large ceramic supply houses and find that by mixing the colors with slip, the product is similar to an opaque underglaze; and that by mixing with glaze, the

product resembles the transparent underglazes. I am not at all sure, though, of the proper proportions of materials to be used for the best working consistency. Any suggestions along these lines would be appreciated.

Try an experiment in which you vary the different items in small amounts, such as 1% increases, and carefully note the various consistencies and other properties. Since your own particular working materials and even the humidity and outside temperature affect the results, this is the only sure way to arrive at a satisfactory answer.

As long as you already are experimenting, you might also try working with glaze stains and body stains in addition to the dry underglaze powders. The stains are much more intense and will give a nice variety of different colors and effects.

What causes a rough, scummy appearance on a transparent cover glaze when used directly over underglaze colors?

Prepared underglaze colors are invariably made with organic gums and brushing mediums which may leave their mark on the cover glaze as they fire out. This can be avoided by firing on the underglaze color before applying the cover glaze.

If the underglaze colors have been applied to greenware, bisque fire before cover glazing. If the colors are applied on bisque, fire the ware when dry to around 1000°F, which is sufficient to burn out the organic materials.

It also may be the color has been applied too heavily or the cover glaze has been underfired.

What causes pinholes in the glaze over an underglaze decoration? Is the glaze or the underglaze at fault when this happens?

If the pinholing appears only over the underglaze, you may assume that the fault is in the procedures controlling the underglaze. The pinholes are caused by gases given off by the underglaze during the firing. These remain in the glaze in the form of bubbles or as pinholes on the surface. To prevent this defect, either bisque fire the ware after it is decorated and before it is glazed, or use a slower firing cycle to allow more time for the gases to escape and the glaze to mature. If the pinholing appears in the glaze when it isn't used over an underglaze, the glaze probably needs more firing time to mature adequately.

I have been attempting to do some majolica-type decoration, using underglaze colors on an unfired, opaque, white glaze. The fired results have been dreadful, with dark, dull colors instead of the crisp, glossy ones I expected. Can you offer any suggestions for getting an attractive result?

You probably are applying too much colorant. If you want to work with pure underglaze, either dry or liquid, you must add enough water until you have a thin solution—a very watery one—before applying it to the unfired white glaze surface. Or you can combine about two parts of underglaze with an equal amount of the glaze you're using, mix these together well, add water, and then apply. Still another formula is to take two parts of underglaze color, add about three parts of a leadless frit, grind these together on a piece of glass, then add water to make a thin solution. If you are brushing the solution on the glaze for a majolica decoration, the addition of a few drops of glycerin will make the material flow onto the dry glaze surface much more easily.

When we brush glaze on underglaze-decorated pieces, we find after firing that the underglaze has run and distorted. What is happening and how can this be prevented?

One cause may be that the underglaze is being distorted when the glaze is brushed on. Spraying the glaze can help avoid this situation, although the best idea is to bisque fire the piece after it is decorated with underglaze and before the glaze is applied. This "sets" the underglaze so that the wet glaze being brushed on will not dissolve and distort it.

Another cause may be that the glaze is attacking the underglaze decoration while it is in the melted state in the kiln. This can be solved by using a covering glaze that is known to be compatible with the underglaze colors. Your local dealer can supply such glazes that are compatible with underglazes and also will fit the body without crazing.

Some of the commercial underglaze colors I use seem to have faded away when they come from the kiln. I have wondered if perhaps they were fired too high and were burning out. I fire to Cone 05. Is this too high?

Prepared underglazes should not burn out at this temperature; most of them will fire much higher. It is probable that your color loss is due to the fact that you are not using enough underglaze color. The best way to learn how to use your materials is to make tests. On a scrap piece of clay, brush several strokes of the color. Go over some of the strokes several times so that you have samples of one, two, three and four coats of color. Glaze and fire these and judge your results.

What would cause a bisque-fired underglaze decoration to disappear in spots after, or during, the transparent glaze firing?

If an underglaze decoration has gone through a bisque firing with success and runs into trouble during glaze firing, then there are strong possibilities that the underglaze and glaze aren't getting along. When the glaze goes into the melted state in the kiln, chemicals in it react with the underglaze and create various problems from complete disappearance to running, spotting, bleaching, etc.

Have you used this glaze before? Try painting various underglaze colors across a test tile in straight lines. Bisque fire; then glaze only half the tile, leaving the remaining half of the underglazed lines exposed. Glaze fire. Now you can check to see if this glaze is reacting unsatisfactorily with the underglaze, because on this single tile you have bisque fired underglaze alone and underglaze which has been glazed.

Lusters

I am seeking information on a rather unusual luster effect in which primarily yellow or gold luster takes on a blue or green (almost fumed) quality. Do you know how this is done?

The effect is traditionally know as cantharides

luster, because it resembles the iridescent wing color of the cantharides beetle. It is created when bismuth and silver chloride are present in a reduction-fired lead glaze, and a variation may be produced in raku.

I want to prepare a silver luster glaze from basic ingredients. Can you provide a recipe for oxidation firing?

Luster glazes for oxidation firing generally consist of a metallic salt, a carbon-producing agent which causes local reduction, and an oil medium. Usually firing in the range from Cone 020 to 018, a typical silver luster consists of 8% silver nitrate dissolved in 32% dammar (a tree resin which will require heating for this purpose) and 60% oil of lavender.

Can you recommend the proper firing temperature for lusters and metals in overglaze work?

Lusters and metals should be fired to a maximum temperature of Cone 018. Pearls and opals are more sensitive and should be fired to slightly below Cone 018; Cone 019 well down is generally better. When subsequent firings of the same piece are required, fire to slightly lower temperatures each time in order to protect the previous coats. For example, if a second coat is required or an application of luster over metal, turn the kiln off when Cone 018 is about one-fourth down. For a third firing of the same piece, fire to a full Cone 019; and a fourth firing to a full Cone 020.

I would like to obtain information about natural ceramic luster glazes, the true metallic salts which are fired in a reducing atmosphere.

Glaze chemist Richard Behrens replied: "I have used the following recipe at Cone 08 as a luster glaze:

Luster Glaze (Cone 08)

Frit 14 (Hommel)	33.8 %
Frit 25 (Pemco)	39.2
Lithium Carbonate	3.9
Flint	23.1
	100.0 %
Add: Copper Carbonate	0.5 %
Bentonite	2.0 %

"Fire in oxidation to Cone 08, then drop the temperature to about 1320°F. Hold the kiln in substantial reduction between this temperature and 1245°F for 20 to 40 or more minutes.

"Copper-silver, copper-bismuth subnitrate, silver-bismuth subnitrate combinations in about 2% amounts give nice lusters. The addition of rutile, stains and other nonmetallic colorants in about 2% amounts often produce modulations in the luster. This is a 1200-year-old Arabian potting technique."

What causes mother-of-pearl luster to appear frosted or crystalline when fired at Cone 018 on a Cone 06 glazed piece of pottery? This does not seem to be a defect in the luster, for I use it successfully on porcelain.

The condition is probably caused by the Cone 06 glaze on which you apply the luster. At Cone 018 the glaze is just beginning to soften and can give the luster a rough surface. Mother-of-pearl and opals are the only lusters likely to be affected this way; when decorating on an 06 glaze, fire to Cone 020 for best results.

Another cause of the frosted appearance would be too heavy an application. The same application on porcelain probably would not give this effect because the glaze remains intact underneath the luster.

Overglaze Enamels

I am very anxious to paint with enamels on porcelain in the manner of the old Chinese Ming wares. Every ceramics supply house that I have tried has only china paints to offer, admitting that these are not the same as enamels. Where can I find real ceramic enamels? Furthermore, how would I apply them?

The term "enamel" in ceramics is a confusing one because it is used loosely to refer to a variety of low-temperature overglaze substances, and also describes the shiny surface quality of any glaze or even of paint. The Germanic roots of the word enamel relate to terms which have to do with melting, hence the broad meaning and use of the word result from broad etymological beginnings.

The term "china paint" is synonymous with the strictest interpretation of the word enamel—as a colored frit or glaze generally firing in a cone range from 022–010. The term may be stretched to also include low-fire (Cone 06–04) glazes applied to higher-fired glazed ware (stoneware or porcelain) and requiring an additional kiln cycle.

Enamels are usually a fritted mixture of colorant, and sometimes an opacifier sold principally as powdered china paint, but also as the copper enamelist's material. Either is traditionally ground on a glass plate mixed with fat oil of turpentine (made by allowing turpentine to stand, leaving a gummy residue). Lavender oil or olive oil are also used as enamel mediums, and these may be thinned to the consistency of oil paint with additions of good quality turpentine. Commercial mediums are also available, as are water-based enamels marketed under the name of "Overstrokes."

Enamels may be made by hand, but because lead is the usual flux, there are certain dangers to the health of both producer and user which require a sound knowledge of glaze chemistry, particularly when these materials might come into contact with food. Even if an enamel is made with acceptable solubility, grinding may increase lead release to an unacceptable level, as will significant variation in firing temperature. These hazards, when considered with the quality of commercial enamels and their relative safety when fired to the recommended cone range, suggest that enamels are best purchased commercially rather than made by the potter.

It is important to apply enamels under dust-free conditions if faults are to be avoided in the fired decoration. Equally important is good ventilation of the kiln during the early stages of the firing when gases are driven off.

Enamel wares during the Ming dynasty typically combined both under- and overglaze decoration. Cobalt blue is the typical underglaze color which bleeds through a soft white glaze. The cobalt decoration was then highlighted with overglaze enamels.

For further information on this topic, see "Overglaze Enamels, Low-Temperature Glazes, and Lusters" in the September 1976 issue of *Ceramics Monthly.*

We have been buying overglazes for decorative work on lamps, finding the contrast between subtle stoneware glazes and bright color to be well received by patrons and customers. But current quantities of production require either that we begin developing our own low-fire recipes or stop using such decoration altogether. Can you suggest a simple base overglaze that might lend itself well to color experimentation?

An excellent, simply formulated recipe which tends toward good stability is:

Enamel Overglaze I (Cone 014)

Frit 3417 (Ferro)	100 parts
Edgar Plastic Kaolin	5
	105 parts

Pemco frit Pb-63 and Hommel 24 may be directly substituted for 3417 in the recipe; all are lead-bearing frits.

Another overglaze recipe is the following smooth, translucent base:

Enamel Overglaze II (Cone 014)

Frit P-25 (Pemco)	56.6 %
Frit P-54 (Pemco)	34.2
Alumina Hydrate	3.2
Kaolin (ASP 400)	6.0
	100.0 %

This composition is lead free. Ferro frit 3819 and Hommel 259 may be substituted for P-25, and Ferro 3134 or Hommel 14 are interchangeable with P-54.

I have been working with china paints, firing at low temperatures (Cone 020), and am searching for a suitable and simple clear formula with very low melting characteristics to use over these. Any suggestions?

Perhaps a good starting point for a very low-firing, simple enamel is the eutectic composition for the PbO-B_2O_3-SiO_2 system: PbO–84%, B_2O_3–12% and SiO_2–4%. This composition reflects the lowest temperature (484°C or 903°F) where these three compounds melt. Potentially toxic in formulation and use, this recipe should only be employed by those with a sound knowledge of ceramic toxicology and studio hygiene.

GLAZE RECIPES

Basics

Any reason why glaze formulas are referred to as recipes? It makes me feel like I'm back in the kitchen.

Even though glaze recipes are often referred to as formulas, the latter description is incorrect. Glaze recipes (also called batch recipes) are lists of minerals used to make a specific batch of glaze. But each mineral may be made up of several chemical compounds. Formulas, on the other hand, are a list of the glaze's chemical ingredients and may be in the form of either molecular formulas, empirical molecular formulas, or percent formulas. A glaze formula might be made with any one of several different recipes depending on the contents of your glaze pantry.

There are many glaze formulas printed in books and magazines listed in percent. How are these changed into gram weights?

Recipes in ceramics are listed by weight unless otherwise stated. Thus the following two recipes are the same:

Yellow Brown Glaze (Cone 6)

Lithium Carbonate	10 %
Albany Slip	90
	100 %

Yellow Brown Glaze (Cone 6)

Lithium Carbonate	10 grams
Albany Slip	90
	100 grams

Additionally the recipe may be multiplied by any number (provided all parts of the glaze are multiplied by the same number) to obtain a useful working batch. For example, multiply the previous recipe times 200 to obtain the following batch recipe—the same glaze:

Yellow Brown Glaze (Cone 6)

Lithium Carbonate	2,000 grams
Albany Slip	18,000 grams
	20,000 grams

It is handy to know that there are 454 grams per pound for estimates. You may wish to round this off to 500 grams per pound because it's easier to remember. The 20,000 gram batch is the same as 44 pounds.

Glaze recipes in *Ceramics Monthly* and other sources often do not state if they are for oxidation or reduction. How is one to know which atmosphere should be used?

Recipes listed in ceramics are typically for oxidation firing unless the recipe states otherwise. Sometimes the reduction term is abbreviated as an "R" or as "Red." Glazes listed for use in oxidation often are quite good in reduction and vice versa. A quick glaze test in with your usual firing is a good idea before mixing a large batch of any glaze. Be sure the test is big enough (3×3 inches minimum), contains texture, and both horizontal and vertical surfaces to see the new glaze in conditions similar to the way it will appear on your forms.

Is there a technically correct or accepted order for listing glaze ingredients in recipes?

Ceramics Monthly lists ingredients in glaze recipes beginning with the fluxes, next contributors of alumina, then refractory materials/silica, finally colorants/opacifiers. Another way to conceive of this order is bases, neutrals, acids, colorants/opacifiers. Each category is listed alphabetically. Compounds which function in more than one category (such as zinc oxide which may be a flux or an opacifier/colorant) are listed according to their purpose.

Low-Fire Glazes

I recently bought at auction a rare little stoneware jug with this glaze formula scratched on the side along with a rust-colored flower: ¾ antimony, ¾ lead, ¾ litharge, ¼ iron rust, ¼ Albany clay. I have always wondered at about what temperature some of our early American pots were fired. Can you tell me at what temperature this specific recipe might have been used?

Glazes prepared with lead and Albany slip clay were widely used in New York or New England potteries from about 1840. These were often fired to 1000°C—approximately Cone 07. Antimony trioxide (a poisonous and volatile material) was the likely compound depicted as antimony, which may have functioned as an opacifier or colorant in this glaze with high lead content.

I am looking for a true orange to coral-red glaze (not the typical copper red one often sees) for use in raku. Do you have access to such a recipe?

There are a number of ways to produce orange to coral-red colors in raku, and these include the use of colorants such as uranium, cadmium and selenium. The following recipe, however, uses chromium oxide in combination with lead to create the color in question.

Orange to Red Raku Glaze

Red Lead	80.3 %
Kaolin	9.2
Flint	10.5
	100.0 %
Add: Chromium Oxide	2.7 %

Such lead-bearing recipes are unsafe for use on containers which might come in contact with food. This glaze is potentially toxic to the potter and user, so it should only be formulated and fired by a ceramist experienced in glaze chemistry and the appropriate handling of toxic materials.

My kiln fires unevenly, something I've learned to live with, and in fact have grown to appreciate the variety of results that can come from a single firing. I work with earthenware, and am wondering if you might have a majolica glaze which can take a three-to-four-cone range from Cone 04 down.

The following leadless recipe is an excellent majolica-style base glaze with broad-range firing capability.

Majolica Base Glaze (Cone 09–04)

Frit 3134 (Ferro)	52.1 %
Kaolin	11.1
Flint	36.8
	100.0 %
Add: Zinc Oxide	15.2 %

If the Ferro frit is not available, Pemco frit P-311 or Hommel frit 90 will substitute.

Could you provide a lead-free recipe for a Cone 06 clear glaze for use with underglazes?

Try the following recipe with your underglazes:

Clear Glaze (Cone 06)

Gerstley Borate	13.3 %
Magnesium Carbonate	10.8
Nepheline Syenite	29.7
Kaolin (ASP 400)	8.5
Flint	37.7
	100.0 %
Add: Zinc Oxide	5.0 %

Of the leadless low-fire recipes, this one is particularly stable due to the many sources of flux it contains. In addition to your use with underglazes, try it also with typical colorant additions for a variety of unusual colors.

Another recipe which should meet your requirements is the following:

Low-Fire Glaze (Cone 06)

Soda Ash	6 %
Frit 3110 (Ferro)	15
Tennessee Ball Clay (10)	30
Bentonite	4
Flint	45
	100 %

This leadless glaze is slightly soluble because of its soda ash content, so make sure it is well mixed each time the batch is used. Even though the same colorant and colorant quantity may be added to both, colors may vary substantially between this recipe and the previous one.

Can you recommend a good quality, nontoxic, shiny white opaque glaze—one which works well with oxide colorants? I am currently firing at Cone 04 in an electric kiln.

Here is a recipe which may meet your needs. It is lead free and achieves its whiteness from the commercial opacifier, Opax.

Boron Gloss White Glaze (Cone 04)

Gerstley Borate ....39.15 %
Ball Clay 18.40
Flint 42.45
100.00 %
Add: Opax ....5.00 %

Colemanite may be substituted directly in this recipe for Gerstley borate, and another opacifier, such as Zircopax, for Opax wherever these glaze compounds are not readily available.

Mid-Range Glazes

I am currently firing at Cone 01, having left Cone 6 for purposes of energy conservation and economy. At the higher temperatures, I used to have a Gerstley borate glaze which fired transparent with milky spots. Can you suggest how such a glaze may be made at Cone 01?

Try the following recipe. It contains no lead and is composed of materials that are readily available at any supplier.

Gerstley Borate Glaze (Cone 01)

Gerstley Borate ....39.2 %
Ball Clay 18.4
Flint 42.4
100.0 %

I'm interested in obtaining a formula (not a recipe) for the kind of glaze applied to commercial porcelain dinnerware. I don't mind if the formula contains lead, and in fact, would prefer it because of the surface consistency typical with lead-fluxed glazes. But I would like the glaze to have very low lead release. What can you suggest?

A typical, low-lead-release formula for "hotel china" is K_2O–0.066, Na_2O–0.179, PbO–0.261, CaO–0.494, Al_2O_3–0.340, B_2O_3–0.314, SiO_2–3.369. When converted to a batch and applied to porcelaneous ware, this glaze fires at Cone 5. Firing conditions will substantially affect lead release, so representative samples should be regularly tested from any production ware.

I am much interested in experimenting with crystalline glazes. I have the use of an electric kiln which fires at

Cone 5. Could you furnish me with a base formula maturing at that cone? Also, I have learned that one must adjust the base glaze to fit different colorants. Could you tell me which glaze elements would probably need such adjustment—possibly those which promote crystallization?

The secret of success is not entirely the formula but the firing and particularly cooling of the glaze. Success lies in hitting the cooling range where the glaze has not entirely stiffened and holding there not minutes, but hours. You can find this by time-consuming experimentation in your kiln. Otherwise you might try normal firing to maturity, and slow cooling to a holding temperature at low red heat by turning switches on and off in your kiln.

You should be able to obtain some pretty nice crystals by cooling slowly the following formula:

Crystalline Glaze (Cone 5)

Lithium Carbonate	8.42 %
Strontium Carbonate	6.73
Titanium Dioxide	7.28
Zinc Oxide	20.02
Nepheline Syenite	20.34
Kaolin	5.82
Flint	31.39
	100.00 %
Add: Copper Carbonate	1.36 %

Additions of about 1% ammonium molybdate and 1% tungstic acid are most useful in providing nuclei upon which crystals will form. Be sure to use firing rings or soft clay biscuit to catch runoff glaze. Crystals form best in runny glazes.

For further information see "Making and Firing Crystalline Glazes" by David Snair in the December 1975 *Ceramics Monthly.*

I am interested in producing the traditional ash-type running glaze in oxidation. Everything I've read indicates that this is only possible in reduction. Can you provide a formula, preferably in the Cone 5–6 range?

Some interesting effects lie between the following two recipes:

Ash Glaze (Cone 5–6)

Any Wood Ash	40%
Local Earthenware or Slip Clay	60
	100%

Ash Glaze (Cone 5–6)

Any Wood Ash	20%
Local Earthenware or Slip Clay	80
	100%

Add 10% red iron oxide to either of these for a richer, more fluxed surface.

I am interested in obtaining a recipe for an easily formulated satin matt glaze to be applied to Cone 6 single-fired ware. Do you have any suggestions?

The following recipe should meet your requirements, but use it on an experimental basis until proper body fit has been established.

Satin Matt Glaze (Cone 6)

Dolomite	20%
Cornwall Stone	60
Ball Clay	20
	100%

I want to move from Cone 9 reduction firing to the Cone 5–6 range in order to save energy and reduce firing costs, and am looking for some recipes from which to start experimentation. What would you suggest?

Joe Cooper of Pincherry Pottery in Worthington, Ohio, has been producing a variety of wares in the Cone 5–6 range for a number of years. One of the bodies he uses is the following:

Stoneware Clay Body (Cone 5–6)

Nepheline Syenite (270 mesh)	14	parts
Cedar Heights Goldart Clay	50	
Cedar Heights Redart Clay	38	
Tennessee Ball Clay (7)	15	
	117	parts
Add: Buff Grog (20 mesh)	11	parts
Bentonite	1	part

Joe comments that "this body has been fired within the range of Cone 4½–8. Cone 8 is probably challenging the body a little. At Cone 6, shrinkage from the wet state to matured (after firing) has varied from about 8–11%. The latter has been consistent in recent firings. Absorption ranges from 2.97% at Cone 4 to 0.84% at Cone 6. The body may be used as ovenware, but should not be used in microwave ovens. Its color is mahogany, somewhat darker in heavy reduction. A typical bisque firing for this clay is to Cone 07 and a normal glaze firing takes approximately eight hours.

"Glazes used with this body include the following:

Transparent, Bright Glaze

(Cone 5–6, oxidation or reduction)

Dolomite	2.63 %
Gerstley Borate	20.01
Whiting	10.29
Zinc Oxide (calcined)	3.84
Custer Feldspar	26.89
Georgia Kaolin (ASP 400)	6.26
Flint	30.08
	100.00 %
Add: Bentonite	1.00 %

Transparent Glaze

(Cone 5–6, oxidation or reduction)

Barium Carbonate	8.47 %
Talc	2.26
Whiting	6.77
Zinc Oxide (calcined)	6.88
Custer Feldspar	45.15
Georgia Kaolin (ASP 400)	5.64
Tennessee Ball Clay (7)	4.29
Flint	20.54
	100.00 %
Add: Bentonite	1.00 %

"When Kona F-4 feldspar is directly substituted for Custer, the recipe above yields a waxy matt. When nepheline syenite is substituted for the Custer feldspar, a satin matt results. The nepheline syenite glaze works best at Cone 5, and this recipe works especially well as onglaze with the Custer feldspar recipe. My practice is to allow the first glaze to dry thoroughly before applying the second. Total thickness of the glaze needs to be considered, as too much will tend to crawl. Controlling thickness for these recipes involves thinning a second glaze coat with a little water before it is applied over glaze. Colorants may be added to these recipes as you like."

I am interested in Cone 6 porcelain glazes, especially a celadon for bringing out incised patterns. Any suggestions?

You might wish to try the following:

Celadon Glaze (Cone 6–7, reduction)

Barium Carbonate	17.2 %
Whiting	7.0
Lepidolite	13.8
Spodumene	25.6
Frit 3134 (Ferro)	13.8
Flint	22.6
	100.0 %
Add: Bentonite	2.0 %
Red Iron Oxide	1.0 %

Firing should proceed to Cone 010 in oxidation, followed by a slowed, moderate reduction to Cone 7. At this point you may cut the burners back, maintaining a reducing atmosphere as the temperature drops to approximately 2095°F, then let the kiln cool normally.

Can you provide a simply formulated satin matt glaze in the Cone 6 range for oxidation firing?

You might be interested in trying the following:

Satin Matt Glaze (Cone 6)

Dolomite	20 %
Cornwall Stone	60
Kaolin	20
	100 %

Another satin matt recipe is:

Satin Matt Glaze (Cone 6)

Whiting	17.0 %
Custer Feldspar	47.0
Kaolin	5.5
Flint	30.5
	100.0 %
Add: Calcined Zinc Oxide	34.8

If this recipe seems too expensive because of the

zinc oxide content, the following recipe may be less costly.

Satin Matt Glaze (Cone 6–8)

Whiting	11.4 %
Talc	2.1
Feldspar (Kingman or Custer)	67.7
Kaolin (ASP 400)	18.4
Flint	0.4
	100.0 %
Add: Zinc Oxide	6.7

We fire in a broad range of temperatures from Cone 06 oxidation to Cone 10 reduction. Is there a clear glaze or a series of clear glazes which will fire across this range?

No single formula will fire from Cone 06 to Cone 10, although there are recipes that have a very broad firing range. Paul Woolery mentions one in the April 1982 issue of *Ceramics Monthly:*

Clear Glaze (Cone 4–10, reduction)

Gerstley Borate	21 %
Wollastonite	8
Nepheline Syenite	30
Kaolin	10
Flint	31
	100 %

An excellent clear glaze, this recipe will fit most stoneware bodies. But in the low-fire range, the best glazes generally contain lead, which may be hazardous to both potter and user (although when properly formulated, fired and handled, lead glazes are safe as is demonstrated by their extensive use in industry). Nevertheless, here are some reliable leadless low-fire recipes—three variations using the same materials in different proportions:

Clear Glaze I (Cone 06)

Frit 3134 (Ferro)	89.5 %
Kaolin	10.5
	100.0 %

Clear Glaze II (Cone 04)

Frit 3134 (Ferro)	79.0 %
Kaolin	21.0
	100.0 %

Clear Glaze III (Cone 1)

Frit 3134 (Ferro)	65.0 %
Kaolin	35.0
	100.0 %

Pemco frit P-54 or Hommel frit 14 may be substituted for Ferro frit 3134 in these recipes. These frits each contain 10.4% Na_2O, 20% CaO, 23.3% B_2O_3 and 43.6% SiO_2. Consequently they are nontoxic and safe to use on ceramic objects which come into contact with food. Try adding colorants to these recipes in typical proportions to produce a variety of new glazes.

High-Fire Glazes

I have lost a favorite oxidation black glaze which does not run or pinhole on porcelain at Cone 9 and fires a rich, smooth black. Could you help?

Try the following recipes:

Black Matt Glaze (Cone 8–10)

Dolomite	23.7 %
Nepheline Syenite	71.6
Kentucky Ball Clay (OM 4)	4.7
	100.0 %
Add: Bentonite	2.8 %
Cobalt Oxide	1.0 %
Iron Oxide	9.0 %
Manganese Dioxide	3.4 %

Shiny Black Glaze (Cone 6–9)

Dolomite	8.76 %
Gerstley Borate	14.65
Whiting	8.92
Cornwall Stone	41.06
Georgia Kaolin	17.85
Flint	8.76
	100.00 %
Add: Black Stain 6600 (Mason)	6.0 %

A number of Japanese folk potters use a kaki red-brown glaze, often contrasted with a gray recipe, and I have seen similar glazes in the U.S. Can you suggest some ingredients for this glaze when fired at Cone 9 in reduction?

Iron-saturated glazes have found their place in the

formularies of many folk potters as well as the contemporary studio potter. Here is a simply formulated recipe worth testing experimentally:

Kaki Red-Brown Glaze (Cone 9, reduction)

Whiting	13 %
Feldspar (Kona F-4)	29
Tennessee Ball Clay (1)	29
Flint	29
	100 %
Add: Red Iron Oxide	15 %

Another variation on this same type of glaze is the following recipe:

Kaki Persimmon (Cone 9, reduction)

Whiting	16.9 %
Feldspar (Kona F-4)	33.7
Edgar Plastic Kaolin	8.4
Flint	41.0
	100.0 %
Add: Red Iron Oxide	12.9 %
Bentonite	1.1 %

I have been looking for a good, simply formulated temmoku glaze which fires in the Cone 9 range. Do you have a potential recipe?

You may be interested in the following recipe which should produce a good temmoku effect:

Temmoku Glaze (Cone 9)

Whiting	2 %
Albany Slip	80
Barnard Clay	10
Nepheline Syenite	8
	100 %

Like most temmoku glazes, this recipe should be applied rather thickly, and may tend to flow.

I am looking for a glaze called Albany Rust for firing at Cone 9 reduction. Have you ever heard of this, and can you provide its recipe?

There are a number of glazes with variations known as Albany Rust, but the following one is perhaps the most common.

Albany Rust Glaze (Cone 9, reduction)

Whiting .... 11 %
Albany Slip Clay 63
Cornwall Stone 26
                                                                    100 %
Add: Bentonite .... 1 %
       Red Iron Oxide .... 5 %

I am interested in obtaining recipes for two ash glazes attributed to the English potter Bernard Leach. One is a kaki, the other is a fat white; both were relatively simple compositions. Can you help?

Two variations of Leach-attributed glazes which fit the description you mention are the following:

Leach White Ash Glaze (Cone 8–10, reduction)

Hardwood Ash .... 10 %
Cornwall Stone 90
                                                                    100 %

Leach Kaki (Cone 9, reduction)

Hardwood Ash .... 36 %
Kona F-4 Feldspar 52
Flint 12
                                                                    100 %
Add: Red Iron Oxide .... 10 %

Bernard Leach probably never used these formulas. If well reduced they look like Leach-style glazes.

In the Summer 1982 issue there was an answer to a question concerning a Kanjiro Kawai glaze; could *Ceramics Monthly* locate another of his recipes (or a glaze that approximates it): Kawai Kaki, a kaki/temmoku?

The following saturated iron glaze is a twin to Kawai Kaki:

Kaki/Temmoku (Cone 9, reduction)

Whiting .... 19.1 %
Zinc Oxide 1.1
Custer Feldspar 33.7
Edgar Plastic Kaolin 7.9
Flint 38.2
                                                                    100.0 %
Add: Bentonite .... 2.3 %
       Copper Carbonate .... 0.6 %
       Red Iron Oxide .... 4.5 %

I am looking for a white glaze and a black glaze that will go together well when fired in reduction on stoneware. My current black and white glazes crawl when one contacts the other. Any help would be appreciated.

A classic black and white combination glaze can be made with the following simply formulated recipe:

Toshiko White Glaze

(Cone 9–10, oxidation or reduction)

Whiting	20 %
Cornwall Stone	20
Kona F-4 Feldspar	40
Georgia Kaolin	20
	100 %
Add: Zinc Oxide	7 %
Bentonite	2 %

To make a black glaze from this semimatt recipe, add 5% cobalt carbonate, 1% manganese carbonate and 20% red iron oxide. Since these glazes have the same base, they should work especially well together.

After a recent brush fire which burned a substantial portion of a nearby grassy meadow, we gathered quite a bit of the ash. After a variety of tests, however, it does not appear to perform like the wood ash we are more used to using in glazes. Can you suggest a grass ash recipe, and tell us why this ash is so different?

Grass ash tends to be high in silica when compared to wood ash, and for this reason it is typically much more refractory. A good recipe for starting experimentation with this potentially useful glaze ingredient is the following:

Grass Ash Glaze

(Cone 10, oxidation or reduction)

Talc	23 %
Whiting	5
Grass Ash	53
Kaolin	13
Flint	6
	100 %

Grass ash may be used in the same manner as wood ash in both the washed and unwashed states—the former removing some of the soluble flux resulting in more mattness of the glaze surface.

Could you suggest a simply formulated glaze for firing at Cone 10? I would like a base recipe to which colorants can be added, composed of relatively inexpensive ingredients.

The following recipe should suit your needs in every respect:

Base Glaze (Cone 10, oxidation or reduction)

Dolomite	20 %
Custer Feldspar	60
Ball Clay	10
Flint	10
	100 %

Any ball clay should work well in this recipe, and those with slightly more iron may tend to produce a slight coloring, particularly in reduction. You may directly substitute other feldspars for the Custer, with minor changes in the surface of the glaze.

I am looking for a good liner to use inside pots being salt glazed—something with a bit of color; not just bland white (and preferably something foolproof enough to withstand the temperature variations typical in my salt firing). Do you know of such a recipe?

Try the following:

Shige's Temmoku Black (Cone 8–11)

Dolomite	5 %
Whiting	6
Kona F-4 Feldspar	67
Edgar Plastic Kaolin	5
Flint	17
	100 %
Add: Cobalt Carbonate	3 %
Red Iron Oxide	5 %
Bentonite	1 %

This glaze produces a handsome iron green with rutilelike flecks, which in a slowly cooling salt kiln can turn to small crystals. It's a classic salt-glaze liner, which fires in a broad range of temperatures and even looks good in narrow spaces where the salt fumes can't reach.

FORMULATING RECIPES
AND CHANGES

Can glazes that are designated for firing in oxidation also be fired in a reducing atmosphere? What changes might be expected in the appearance of the glaze?

Glazes that work well in oxidation will often be good reduction glazes. Some oxidation glazes are much improved by reduction, but there may be changes in glaze color and texture, particularly when iron and/or copper are present in the formula. Your clay body may also play a more significant role in influencing glaze color when body colorants become more active in reduction. Some reduction glazes make good formulas for oxidation, too.

Should the specific gravity of glaze be changed when used for single-fire ware? If so, will you provide some figures?

Glaze applied directly on greenware for single firing generally has a specific gravity ranging from 1.430 to 1.470, while batches designed for application to bisque may range from 1.460 on relatively porous surfaces, to 1.700 on very hard bisque.

Ceramic glazes and bodies apparently come in a variety of hardnesses, as I notice that there is a difference in abrasion resistance from one glaze to the next, particularly in the dinner plates I make. What causes hardness in glazes, and what can I do to make glazes harder and more resistant to abrasion?

Hardness in ceramic materials results primarily from the strength of the bond between atoms of the substances. Among the more durable materials in ceramics, the following ones are rated from hardest to softest: SiC, Al_2O_3, ZrO_2, SiO_2. The traditional way to increase glaze hardness is to add alumina (Al_2O_3), and this is usually done in the form of a clay addition. We don't typically add the harder SiC because it tends to bubble strongly and causes local reduction wherever it is fired.

Geologists are familiar with Moh's scale—a system

of testing based on the known hardness of various pure rocks (listed here from softest to hardest): 1–talc, 2–gypsum, 3–calcite, 4–fluorite, 5–apatite, 6–feldspar, 7–quartz, 8–topaz, 9–corundum, 10–diamond. Ceramic glazes can be test scratched with the materials of Moh's scale to determine their hardness rating (if the glaze can be scratched by quartz, then it is not as hard as 7; if it can be still scratched by feldspar, then it is not as hard as 6, etc.). The hardest porcelains (Cone 15) tend to have a hardness between that of pure orthoclase feldspar and quartz.

According to Russell Utgard, geology professor at the Ohio State University, empirical testing of glazes—scratching them with various minerals—will help to establish a standard for comparison. For consistent analysis, scratch in the same manner with the same surface of the test rock. Variation in the crystalline structure of some minerals could result in different ratings with different contact points.

Glazes which come in contact with metal tableware ought to be sufficiently hard as to not be scratched by the action of a knife and fork. Glazes and bodies which tend to be porous are additionally susceptible to abrasion from such implements: a soaking period at peak temperature during firing often helps to eliminate glaze bubble porosity in dinnerware, as does the avoidance of sulfur in the body, carbonates and other gas producers in the glaze.

I have been reading about the toxic effects of barium carbonate. Can you tell me how much barium sulfate can be substituted—specifically in reduction glazes?

In order to get the same amount of barium from barium sulfate as in a recipe calling for barium carbonate, you will need 1.18 parts of the sulfate for each 1 part of the carbonate (multiply the amount of barium carbonate in the recipe times 1.18). Some glazes are completely unaffected by this change, but other recipes are profoundly affected by the presence of sulfates—sometimes for the better, sometimes for the worse. Nevertheless, it is worth making the barium sulfate substitution experimentally in some test batches to see if you like the results.

a glossy glaze that I would like to change to a
oth matt. Can you help?

One method of matting a glaze is to increase the
calcium content in the formula. Common sources of
calcium include whiting and wollastonite.

I have a glaze that I'm quite fond of, but it tends to run off the pot. Is there a general solution to making glazes less fluid?

Most glazes can be made less fluid simply with an
addition of kaolin (5–10%), and often with no difference in the other physical properties of the recipe.

I am currently firing a simple Cone 06 glaze composed of 50% Ferro frit 3419 and 50% white earthenware clay— the latter being the same as I use for throwing. Although it is an excellent glaze, my kiln fires unevenly, causing ware on some shelves to be under- or overfired. Is there something I can add to the recipe which will broaden its firing range?

Glazes composed of few materials tend to have this
problem. Increasing the sources of flux is one way to
broaden glaze firing range. Try adding 5% whiting.

I would like to glaze mullite kiln shelves, but have been unable to find or adjust a formula to do the job without crazing. Could you provide a Cone 10 or 11 recipe that would work?

Mullite kiln shelves tend to shrink very little during
firing and therefore most typical glazes will not fit
properly. A low-shrinkage, lithium-containing glaze
recipe is:

Low Shrinkage Glaze (Cone 11)

Petalite	77 %
Talc	14
Whiting	3
Kaolin	6
	100 %

Although designed to mature at Cone 11, this
batch may also mature in the Cone 10 range. The
whiting content could be increased in 5% increments
until the desired Cone 10 melt is achieved, or the
addition of sufficient amounts of most metallic oxide

colorants could also lower the maturing point.

Your own glazes may be modified for reduced shrinkage by exchanging lithium-containing compounds for other glaze fluxes.

I've been experimenting with oxidation-fired glazes in the stoneware range, but find my results are just not up to snuff. I've seen beautiful oxidation-fired glazes formulated by others and figure there surely must be some basic advice or guidelines for developing these. What do you recommend?

There are thousands of ways that suitable oxidation-fired glazes can be formulated, so consider the following generalities as starting points for developing good glazes on stoneware: 1) Many of the best oxidation-fired glazes are based on Albany slip or some other complex, secondary, surface clay (Barnard slip, Michigan slip, red earthenware, etc.). That is, they have a large amount of Albany sliplike clay in the glaze formula—70% to 90% by weight. Try using and altering such recipes, or develop your own such glazes (by adding one or two glaze materials to Albany slip) which tend to have interesting and diverse surface/coloring. 2) Many of the best oxidation effects commonly result from layering glazes one on top of another. Try this with your current glazes, layering up to four glazes deep. Severely thinning each batch allows for the extra coats of glaze without encouraging crawling from excessive glaze surface tension. 3) Dipping and spraying are usually the most productive oxidation glaze application processes, because such glazes generally show every nuance of thickness which is achieved more evenly using these methods. 4) Another approach to discovering recipes which are especially useful in oxidation is to seek those high in barium and magnesium, as the matt surfaces produced by these fluxes, and the color reaction with common colorants, can be both handsome and unusual. Ceramists should note cautions regarding the safe use of potentially toxic materials such as soluble barium compounds before formulating with this glaze flux. 5) When using colorants in oxidation glazes, metallic carbonates and commercial stains are preferred because they generally disperse better than oxides, thus avoiding a kind of colorant acne, which is often offensive visually. In addition, it is useful to mill or screen oxidation glazes in the wet state in order to ensure the further dispersal of the glaze's constituents. 6) Finally, try developing crystalline glazes, the rococo royalty of the oxidation glaze family. For further information on these, see Cameron Covert's article "Crystal Glazes" in the September 1985 *Ceramics Monthly*.

After several years of firing to Cone 9 reduction, I am one of the legions switching over to Cone 6 oxidation. My problem is that I can't seem to come up with a really first-rate basic glaze for onglaze brushed decoration at Cone 6. I want a glaze that has some life to it—ideally a fat, white, waxy matt to semigloss. I have tested many recipes but have come up with only two that come close; however, there is some slight surface movement with both, and this fuzzes the lines of brushwork. For your information, these glazes are:

Paul's White Glaze (Cone 6)

Gerstley Borate	15.7 %
Talc	8.6
Whiting	12.0
Custer Feldspar	43.0
Edgar Plastic Kaolin	8.6
Flint	12.1
	100.0 %
Add: Zircopax	8.1 %

Cushing Satin Matt Glaze (Cone 6)

Whiting	20 %
Frit 3124 (Ferro)	25
Nepheline Syenite	25
Edgar Plastic Kaolin	15
Flint	15
	100 %
Add: Zircopax	10 %

In the case of the first glaze, I realize that it may be the Gerstley borate that is causing the slight surface movement; in fact, this was a Cone 9 reduction glaze which I modified to Cone 6 by adding Gerstley borate. Both of these recipes have nice, fat, somewhat shiny surfaces—superior altogether to the typical, dead Cone 6 oxidation glazes. Am I looking for something that doesn't exist? Is it perhaps the case that to get a lively, somewhat shiny glaze in oxidation, one is inevitably going to have some surface movement?

You ought to be able to adjust either of these recipes to take onglaze decoration without surface movement, and there are a variety of ways to do that. An increase in flint is one simple method, but this may change the glaze fit. If so, try increasing the Edgar Plastic Kaolin content for a less drastic change in glaze fit. Or, decrease the quantity of Gerstley borate. In each of these cases, 3% increments should be sensitive enough to give you the results you seek. Better yet, leave these good glazes alone, and apply decoration with strong colorants under the glaze instead of onglaze; with this method the decoration usually will remain where you put it.

Is there a simple method for lowering the firing temperature of Cone 8–9 glazes for firing at Cone 6?

Many Cone 8–9 glazes will fire without alteration at Cone 5 or 6, although matt glazes tend to become more stony, and high gloss recipes tend to appear more matt. But if more of the original surface quality of the Cone 8–9 glaze is required, a one-for-one substitution of nepheline syenite for the feldspar portion of the recipe may be sufficient.

GLAZE DEFECTS

Crawling

A glaze I've been using for years has started to crawl, and I'm wondering if you could suggest some possible causes for this defect.

Crawling, the pulling together of glaze into separate lumps, sometimes with exposed body between, can be the result of a variety of causes. Dust, grease or oil (from one's skin or from contact with food) on the bisque resists the glaze's ability to adhere to the body. Glazes with substantial amounts of feldspar, zinc or other opacifiers may tend to crawl because large amounts of these materials tend to increase glaze viscosity, which is at the heart of this defect. A batch milled too finely or applied too thickly may encourage crawling. Excessive clay in the glaze may cause the material to shrink more than the bisque, creating fault lines in the glaze coating which help to instigate crawling, particularly when the previously mentioned high-viscosity materials are included in the batch.

Glazes containing slightly soluble ingredients, such as wood ash, colemanite or Gerstley borate, may tend to crawl after thickening (flocculation) during storage. Attempts to thin the batch usually raise the water content so much that the glaze coat cracks as it dries on the pot. Subsequent firing may result in crawling, or may even cause globs of glaze to "jump" off the pot and land on the shelf.

I have been having problems with glaze crawling away from the edges of slip decoration during Cone 10 firings. (The pots were slip decorated prior to bisquing.) I have tried wetting the bisque, but nothing seems to work. Can you help?

The cause of crawling is often hard to pinpoint. Slips which are highly refractory may prevent glaze from bonding to the pot during firing; adding a small amount of flux (such as whiting) to a dry slip will encourage better adhesion. Bisque temperature can also be a factor. If ware is too absorbent from a low bisque, it may take on excessive water from the glaze, resulting in shrinkage cracks through the glaze coat. This may lead to crawling, as will too thick an application of glaze, especially when one glaze is used over another for decorative purposes. Taking a close look at the dried glaze surface and powdering any cracks with your finger may help. Another frequently overlooked cause of crawling is too much moisture in the kiln during the early stages of firing. If heat rises too quickly in the kiln during the early stages of firing, moisture in the glaze may be driven out too rapidly, weakening the glaze coat as well as its bond with the body. Other common causes of crawling include dust or oil on bisqueware, use of highly viscous glazes, excessive raw zinc (substitute calcined zinc), nonhomogeneous clay bodies, or over-grinding of the glaze batch.

The problem that has been plaguing me lately is crawling around cobalt decoration. Can you explain the cause and help solve this defect?

Mixing cobalt oxide with glaze as if it were a slip for underglaze decoration is not such a good idea. The uneven appearance of your blue decoration can be traced in part to cobalt oxide not being completely dispersed. Further, the cobalt/glaze coloring material melts at a much lower temperature than the base glaze because cobalt is a strong flux. Thus, this material used for decoration is significantly overfired, creating further boiling, crawling and blistering around the decoration.

The solution to your problem is to substitute 1½ parts cobalt carbonate for each part of cobalt oxide used, because the weaker carbonate will disperse much more completely. Additionally, instead of using glaze as slip, mix the cobalt with slip made from the body (adjusted with increments of ball clay if you have problems getting it to fit properly). This will render the cobalt less reactive with the glaze and help reduce its strong fluxing tendency. If you still get boiling, craters and pinholes in the decoration, simply cut back on the amount of cobalt carbonate in your decorating slip until the problem disappears.

Crazing

What causes crazing and how do I alter a recipe or the firing/cooling cycle to stop this glaze fault?

Crazing is an effect with a variety of similar causes. Parmelee and Harman, in their text *Ceramic Glazes*, list five types of crazing according to cause: thermal shock, stress, frost, moisture and firing (the kiln). The type most commonly discussed is firing or kiln crazing, which results from a poor fit between glaze and body. Because of the nature of silica, adding flint to either glaze or clay tends to reduce crazing, provided the free silica content of the body does not exceed 20%. The best glaze fit is in slight compression.

Because glaze is actually a glass, like glass it can crack under certain circumstances. Thus it is in service that we see the other types of crazing appear. Thermal shock crazing results from the ware being heated and cooled, like a casserole in use. A number of tests are mentioned in ceramic literature to determine a propensity to develop this type of crazing. One suggests that the ware should be able to withstand ten cycles of being heated from 250°F (120°C) in dry air to immersion in 68°F (20°C) water, without crazing.

Moisture crazing is, as one would expect, the result of expansion caused by moisture in the ware, and also may be determined by the previously mentioned test.

Stress crazing is seen most often in tile but may occur in other ceramic applications. In the former, stress is applied by the setting of tile mortar, creating the characteristic stretch crazing in which the cracks are parallel.

Frost crazing results from the freezing and thawing of the ware which causes the same natural expansion and contraction that turn rocks to clay.

Sometimes crazing is a delayed process which takes place over a period of years, and the amount of time for crazing to appear depends upon the amount of fit differential between glaze and body and the hardness of the glaze.

Some current literature suggests that crazing may be related to kiln cooling speed. Improperly formulated bodies may appear to be in better condition than in the long run through slow cooling because they were eased through quartz inversion, but the stress of the poor glaze/body fit remains and will eventually appear. Fast cooling appears to speed the presence of crazing which would otherwise develop as delayed crazing. There is a relationship, however, between the time allowed the glaze in high heat, and for this reason a soaking period at the peak firing temperature allows more silica to be dissolved into the glaze and thus helps reduce the tendency to craze. Insofar as slow cooling allows extra silica to move from the crystalline to the liquid/glassy state, it may help.

Opening the kiln before it is sufficiently cool will sometimes create thermal shock crazing and even dunting (breakage) of the ware in the same way that a glass bottle might crack if cooled too quickly, and this complicates the issue of slow cooling. Fast cooling during quartz inversion can also be a factor, but there is no evidence to support that typical kiln cooling cycles are inherently insufficient.

Do you have any suggestions about "firing down" an electric kiln that cools too fast? I want to eliminate crazing that I get whenever glazes cool too rapidly.

Most kilns, with insulating fiberbrick walls from 2½ to 3 inches thick, and particularly those with only refractory fiber insulation, will usually turn out glazes with less flaws if some firing down is applied. A basic firing-down schedule begins with about half an hour on medium or on the midpoint setting as soon as the kiln reaches peak temperature. Some potters extend this soaking period as long as four hours in order to allow gases to come out of solution, to eliminate craters and pinholes, and especially to encourage the growth of micro- and macrocrystalline patterns which break up and make the visual texture of oxidation glazes more interesting. Beyond this, the kiln can be put on low settings until the cooling decline ceases, thereafter letting the kiln cool at its own rate. Insofar as these measures dissolve silica from the clay body into the glaze/body interface, they help to eliminate crazing. But whenever the shrinkage differential between body and glaze is too great, crazing is only delayed by a slow cooling—such works will craze later anyway. Since this shrinkage differential is the most common cause of crazing, try adding silica to your glaze before attempting a standard firing-down schedule that may prove time consuming and bothersome. Start by adding 2% increments of flint up to a 10% addition to the dry glaze batch weight. Repeatedly subject the test tiles to heat stress by going from room temperature to boiling water and back to room temperature to see which glazes will not craze under such stresses.

Devitrification

A glaze I have been firing for a period of years has recently been coming from the kiln with a new, sugary, crystallized quality. Can you explain this and suggest a cure?

Provided the glaze ingredients are the same, and there has been no substantial change in the recipe's chemical composition, it appears that your glazes are devitrifying (the glass changes to a crystalline state). Glazes which have large quantities of silica are prone to this problem when cooled slowly. So try cooling faster from the time the kiln is shut off, either by leaving the damper partly ajar on a fuel-burning kiln, or by removing peepholes and/or slightly opening the door/lid on an electric kiln. Use common sense to avoid circumstances where such procedures might be fire hazards or cause cracking. Faster cooling may produce significant color shifts, and generally colors are brighter with faster cooling.

What happens chemically during glaze devitrification, and how can this be controlled? Is there anything that can be done with a whole kiln full of such ware?

Devitrification is a phenomenon which occurs during cooling of the kiln, and in which the glaze components separate from the fluid state to form micro-and macrocrystals. Both zinc silicate and calcium borate types are common. Even if the glaze does not appear to contain sufficient materials for devitrification, they may be leached from the clay body. Decreasing the alumina or silica content (or both) may be helpful in controlling devitrification; lowering calcium, barium, magnesium, zinc or similar oxides may also succeed. While devitrification may produce interesting effects, quantities of undesirably devitrified ware can sometimes be salvaged by refiring to a higher temperature.

General Troubleshooting

I have tried a variety of published glaze formulas and find that many don't work. Am I doing something wrong or is there something else altering the stated results?

Glaze formulas should be considered experimental—
the potter should always test a small batch before extensive use. There are a number of factors at work in
glaze formulation: From time to time there are
substantial differences in materials as they are supplied across the country—both particle size (mesh)
and composition are involved, and these factors
have a major effect. In addition, water is perhaps
the most variable of raw materials—quite pure in
some regions, and loaded with minerals in others.
Altitude, humidity, speed of firing, thickness of
application, and contributions from various clay
bodies all affect the results. Potters who have moved
long distances often tell of a new glaze batch made
in the same way and applied in the same manner
reacting with completely different results in the new
location.

**My supplier changed sources of one glaze compound
which I use constantly in two favorite recipes. The new
material appears more coarsely ground, is of somewhat
different color, and my glazes have become much more
matt on firing. Does particle size of glaze material affect
the color of the compound and fired results?**

Particle size will affect the color of some ceramic
compounds, as can be proved by experimentally
screening and separating successively finer mesh
batches of a material such as rutile. In addition, it may
be generally stated that smaller particle sizes of ceramic materials will yield lower melting temperatures
in the glaze batch. It is important to maintain the
same source of supply to achieve consistent results.

**I have been having trouble with crystals forming in my
glaze during cold weather. They only happen when I'm
less active in the studio and the glaze often sits for days
without being used or stirred. Could you tell me what
ingredient(s) is/are causing this and suggest a substitution? Or, if no reformulation is possible, perhaps you
know some other way to keep this from happening. My
glaze contains Gerstley borate, lithium carbonate, whiting, Custer feldspar, nepheline syenite, Edgar Plastic
Kaolin, silica and Zircopax. Strangely enough, screening
out these crystals hasn't made any difference in the fired**

look of the glaze. How come?

You've been finding the characteristic six-sided sodium silicate crystals in your glaze. Leaving the batch unstirred, particularly in cold weather, causes the crystals to come out of solution because the batch is supersaturated with both silica and sodium in their soluble forms. The reason the glaze seems unaffected is because sodium silicate steals from both the glass former and the flux section of the glaze, thus tending not to influence melt on many recipes. Heating the batch and restirring will cause the sodium silicate crystals to return to solution (you can heat just the strained crystals and water on a hot plate, then pour this liquid back into the glaze batch). Substitution of a frit for the Gerstley borate and some of the silica should help lower the soluble sodium content enough to reduce or prevent crystal formation. Try experimenting with substituting frits that resemble Gerstley borate: Ferro frit 3227, Pemco frit P-878 (which contains zirconium—thus reduce the Zircopax somewhat) and Pemco frit P-1N72. Formulas for these were published in the article "Frit Formulas," which appeared in the May 1978 *Ceramics Monthly.*

I recently moved from a coastal state to a mountain location, and find that there is a significant difference in my glazes. Could the change in atmospheric pressure be affecting them or is there some other problem?

The pressure change from sea level to high altitude is not sufficient to affect most glazes, but the significant change which resulted from your new geographical location is in the composition of the atmosphere. Of importance is the amount of moisture present during firing, which can affect both cone and glaze, depending upon the materials used to compose them. Changes in the mineral content of the water supply can also have a noticeable effect, and high-altitude firing can change the draft characteristics of fuel-burning kilns.

Can different types of water affect a glaze? I have mixed Cone 6 recipes at our potters' guild in the city, using the softened tap water, and the glazes have worked well.

When I mixed the same recipes at my house in the country, using hard well water, they ran excessively. What can be done to correct this?

It should be determined that the materials in your studio are identical to the ones at the guild, and that they are properly labeled and pure. Where groups of potters have access to the same glaze pantry, compounds are sometimes contaminated. Your firing method, schedule, and use of pyrometric cones should be compared with that of the guild's and adjusted if necessary. The proposed cause of the glazes' fluidity can be checked by using some of the city water with your raw materials, fired in your kiln. If the results are comparable to those at the guild, then the water appears to be the culprit. Hard or well water can contain large amounts of minerals, such as calcium or iron, and these could cause excess glaze flow. By experimentally decreasing fluxes in the recipe, the problem may be corrected.

I have been using some brightly colored ceramic glazes which when fired in my electric kiln come out perfectly, but when fired in an oxidation atmosphere in my larger gas kiln, the colors are rendered rather dull and faded, even when I match firing cycles exactly. What's the cause of this, and how can I get brighter colors in the gas kiln?

It may not be possible to achieve the results you seek, because gas kilns, even when firing in complete oxidation, produce a sizable quantity of water vapor, which has been shown to dull a variety of brightly colored ceramic glazes. For this reason, industrial ceramists have turned to electric kilns as there is no reasonable way to stop the formation of water vapor— a by-product of combustion in fossil-fueled (especially natural gas) kilns.

We have been firing at Cone 01 in an electric kiln, producing glazed redware, and lately, because of a change in frit, have felt the need to raise firing temperature in order to make our glazes flow a little more. But even after an increase of two cones, I am amazed that there is no difference in the appearance of the fired ware. Can you suggest a solution to making these glazes more fluid?

Using small cones in a relatively fast-firing electric kiln, there are only 2 degrees difference between Cone 01 and Cone 2 at a 540°F rate of temperature increase per hour. There is in fact no difference at this rate between small Cones 1 and 2! Thus, even though the cone numbers sound like an extraordinary rise, changing from Cone 01 to Cone 2 is a small increase. Try firing at Cone 3 or 4 to obtain the results you seek.

Is there any way to remove a piece of kiln wash from the glazed inside surface of a bowl? I made the mistake of applying kiln wash on both sides of my kiln shelves, and naturally a piece of the wash dropped onto one of my pots during the firing.

Try using an electric grinding wheel (or a Dremel tool with a carborundum tip) to remove as much wash as possible. The scar will still be there, but you might salvage the work by reapplying the same glaze over the spot or applying an opaque glaze over the existing glaze and refiring. Protect yourself from breathing kiln wash dust during grinding by wearing an appropriate respirator.

I was supplied with a product known locally as "synthetic" colemanite. When mixed in my recipes it caused the glaze to leap from the ware in all directions, no matter how little had been added to the batch. Can you tell me what is the cause of this problem and how it can be avoided?

Such glaze problems can be eliminated by switching to Gerstley borate. It appears that your "synthetic" colemanite contains some larger crystals of calcium borate which are capable of decrepitating (exploding) when heated. If you wish to continue the use of this type of colemanite, a considerably finer state of this chemical might overcome this problem. Before use, grind the "synthetic" colemanite in a ball mill.

In firing some alkaline glazes (which use soda ash), I have been getting unpleasant effects. The glaze appears very dull and rough, yet I have seen the same glazes as used by other potters come out smooth and glossy. In comparing firing notes with them, I just can't figure out what I am doing that is wrong. Can you offer any suggestions?

The alkaline fluxes are extremely soluble and it is

quite possible that your bisque is fired too low. If so, it is quite porous and absorbs some of the flux, leaving an incomplete glaze on the surface. Try firing your bisque to a higher temperature so that it will not be quite as porous.

Do you have any suggestions for controlling the flow of a very fluid glaze? I have a fine glaze that produces a beautiful blue and brown striated effect, but it is so runny that it literally flows off the bottom of the pot. I have tried changing the formula to correct this fault, but I also lost the unique textural effect. Is there any other approach to solving this problem?

You might try using a lighter application of glaze near the bottom of the pot, and the usual heavy application on the upper areas. Or you might want to go to the trouble of making a thrown clay support that fits the bottom of the pot and catches the excess glaze that flows off the pot. This process was discussed and illustrated in "Making and Firing Crystalline Glazes" by David Snair in the December 1975 *Ceramics Monthly*.

One of my stoneware glazes gives spectacular results, provided the firing temperature is exact, but tends toward craters, blisters and pinholing when under- or overfired. Can you explain this?

Glazes which tend to be viscous at the peak firing temperature are among the most handsome, and include a great many of the higher firing recipes. But viscous glazes are also prone to effects sometimes thought of as defects when under- or overfired. In the case of underfiring, gases are still bubbling from the glassy melt and are captured in that state. If overfired, too much heat creates corrosive reactions between the glaze and the clay body, releasing additional gas which bubbles through the glaze, leaving further blisters or pinholes.

It may help to substitute oxides in your recipe for carbonates, sulfates and nitrates. Holding peak firing temperature for approximately one-half hour may lessen all gas-related glaze faults.

Why do my glazed bowls consistently look better on the inside, even though the same glaze is used overall, and

applied by pouring and dipping in exactly the same way?

First, check your glazing technique. Most often interiors are glazed first, and liquid from this coat is absorbed into the body. The absorbed moisture may affect the thickness of the exterior coat, thus altering fired appearance.

Additionally, glazes give off gases from their volatile materials during firing, and these reactive materials often are trapped inside ceramic forms, influencing the inside surfaces. The outside of the pot is typically swept by draft in a gas firing, but even in an electric firing there is a regular exchange of atmosphere around the pots caused by air entering and leaving through the cracks between kiln sections, and through the top peephole (which is typically left unplugged during electric firing). Firing ware in closed saggars nearly the size of each piece will equalize the differences, if that is your wish, although this seems an extreme step. Or you may be able to experimentally adjust the recipe of the glaze used on the exterior by increasing its volatile materials content (typically fluxes and coloring oxides) to produce the desired result.

Why, when I use Zircopax, Ultrox or tin in a glaze, does the glaze come out bubbly? Large, blistery bubbles form whenever I use any of the above opacifiers, both in recipes calling for these or in other glazes I am trying to opacify. These glazes otherwise perform beautifully.

Zircopax, Ultrox and tin, in addition to being opacifiers, also act as refractory materials in the glaze; that is, they tend to raise the melting point of the batch to which they are added. During the cycle of the glaze melt, the batch gives off gas prior to settling down at its proper temperature; this gas results from the breaking down of oxides and carbonates, etc. as they form the new compounds required to make a durable glass. Some glazes bubble more than others during this period, some bubble closer to the appropriate firing temperature for that specific glaze. When sufficient refractory materials are added (such as these opacifiers) the bubbling range can spill over into the old proper firing range, requiring either that the glazes be fired hotter, or that additional flux be added to the glaze to overcome the refractory opacifiers. In 5% increments, try adding more of whatever material currently fluxes each of your various glazes until a new equilibrium is found.

After trying Richard Behrens's basalt clay bodies that were published in the June 1975 issue, I found the most workable at Cone 6 was "Basalt Body III," substituting Red Horse Clay (or Alberhill) for the red clay:

Basalt Body III (Cone 6)

Manganese Dioxide	6 %
Nepheline Syenite	2
Red Iron Oxide	16
Bentonite	3
Red Clay	40
Kaolin	18
Kentucky Ball Clay (OM 4)	15
	100 %

I tried the body substituting local sewer pipe clay for the red clay, which also worked well, but had difficulty in glazing. Even experimenting with several Cone 6 recipes, I got craters and large pinholes and the clay sometimes cracked during cooling, even a day or two after firing. Unglazed, the basalt body works well. Any help in solving this problem would be greatly appreciated.

The basalt body has different properties from the "normal" potting body and is somewhat similar to Parian with its high flux content. Basalt is usually used in the unglazed state because of its tendency to be self-glazing, and this is the result of large quantities of iron and manganese oxides, which also release significant oxygen that may cause blisters, pinholes or craters. A lack of "fit" can cause the cracking. Because of the unusual body composition, a normal glaze would probably not do for basaltware. But the following recipe may be used as a base for experimentation:

Glaze for Basaltware (Cone 015)

Frit 3134 (Ferro)	26.4 %
Frit 25 (Pemco)	43.6
Lithium Carbonate	9.9
Kaolin	6.1
Flint	14.0
	100.0 %

This is applied to a Cone 6 fired pot and subsequently refired to Cone 015.

We have a salt-glazed planter in which a plant recently died even though it had received reasonable care. I can't help but wonder if the planter wasn't at fault. What do you think?

We tested soil from your planter and found an extremely high level of soluble salts—nearly twice the level at which plants are normally stunted or killed. Additionally, the outside of the planter had acquired, over a period of months, a fine coating of soluble salt residue. Our feeling is that the plant was indeed killed by salt from the planter which may have remained on the bottom of the piece after firing or even in the wall of the planter which has proved to be rather porous. It is important for those who salt glaze planters to see that the body is vitreous (draw tiles are a good way to check this during firing), and to make sure the firing chamber is reasonably clear of salt before the kiln is shut off and/or closed up for cooling.

Ceramist Charles Lakofsky saw this problem as part of a larger one—glazes in which oxides, particularly the soluble alkalies, have not been dissolved in the ultimate glass and which therefore are still soluble. He commented, "When I was at the Cleveland Art School, way back when, we used a raw glaze compound of borax, baking soda, feldspar, clay and flint, fired to Cone 012. It gave some beautiful colors, particularly copper blues and chrome lemon yellows, but it crazed like mad. As with bodies fired to that cone, it couldn't help but be porous and these pots leaked like sieves. After being around a while, particularly if used as planters, salt efflorescence would bloom along the craze marks. This is probably the same problem with your planter.

"I have sometimes seen work taken from the kiln with an actual flow of melted salt inside the pot where it had fallen during firing and simply had not volatilized. I wonder if such a lack of insoluble glassiness might also be due to too low a firing temperature at which point silica in the body is simply not hot enough to be chemically active.

"In my notes from Clarence Merritt's glaze class at Alfred, I find the following: Soluble materials are not made insoluble by merely melting, but must be in combination with other substances which will form insoluble silicates such as the alkaline earths, lead, zinc and clay. It is a good idea to keep the amount of alkali to 0.5 equivalent, with the upper limit at 0.6; to go beyond this might give a glass which is still soluble. The oxides combining with soluble oxides to render them insoluble are called counteracting bases. It is best to use at least two counteracting bases, one of which may be Al_2O_3. To keep balance between bases and acids and within the range of easy fusion, the ratio between RO and RO_2 groups should be kept between 1:1 and 1:3, the average being 1:1.5 or 1.2. If the ratio falls below 1:1, the glaze will be dry—without fusion. All of this is theoretical, but the solubility of salt glazes may be based on this."

The leaching of soluble materials can be a special problem to the functional potter, particularly where drainage is not included in planters such as the one in question. Plants can sometimes be salvaged where such drainage exists by allowing the soil to dry out, then watering thoroughly until water drains out the bottom of the pot, then water again allowing excess water to drain, then water again. This should remove much of the excess salt. When the soil dries out again, follow the same procedure.

After using a set of dinnerware for more than a year, I noticed that the stoneware glaze surface appears to be deteriorating on plates which were used more often and repeatedly washed in the dishwasher. Is it possible that the dishwasher detergent can attack the glaze, causing this pitting? Is there some way to test if this is the case? Are there any types of glazes resistant to this defect?

Dishwasher detergents, because of their high alkalinity, may attack ceramic glaze when it is improperly formulated: that is, the glass produced is not particularly durable or is slightly soluble. Glazes containing large amounts of boron or low alumina and silica are particularly suspect. A traditional test in industry is to weigh a completely dry piece of ware, then boil it for six hours in a 3% solution of sodium phosphate or sodium carbonate, thereafter *completely* drying the plate and reweighing it on a sensitive scale to determine if any material has been lost in the interim. It is important that the plate be completely dried before each weighing by heating sufficiently to drive off all moisture held in pores of the ware. Because reactions with sodium phosphate or carbonate may deposit products of reaction in the glaze pores (masking weight loss of the glaze itself), this test is a general one and not entirely foolproof. Commercial laboratory testing can be more definitive, where necessary. (See "Frit Formulas" in the May 1978 *Ceramics Monthly* for lab addresses; contact your local health department or state industrial safety department for further information on testing ware.)

Recipes containing lithium materials and zirconium oxide tend to resist detergent attack, demonstrating greater durability than those without these compounds.

While glaze composition is one factor in the deterioration of glaze surface through detergent attack, the composition of the detergent itself may vary in corrosiveness to glaze.

THE STUDIO

EQUIPMENT

Ball Mills

I have a quantity of large ball bearings, and wonder if these can be used in place of the porcelain pebbles in my ball mill. Will this have any effect on the glaze?

Large ball bearings may be used in a ball mill and should not contribute significantly to glaze color. However, they will tend to reduce milling time because of their additional weight.

Is there any way that I could compound glazes that call for ball milling, even though I don't own a ball mill? I don't want to invest in any equipment that I don't need or have room for, but I don't like to be limited in the glaze recipes I want to try. I'd appreciate knowing if there is any substitute method I could use.

If the recipes don't call for a long period of milling, you could try mixing small amounts of the glaze by hand in a mortar and pestle, then screening it through a 100-mesh screen. If you don't have the screen, you may want to make your own "ball mill." Take a glass jar with a tight-fitting lid and fill it about one-third full with glass marbles. Then add the glaze (not too full), cover and shake. Because the batch will absorb more of the water as it is "milled," you can add a small bit of water to the jar and marbles after you have emptied out the glaze; swish it around to clean off the equipment and save the residual glaze to add to your batch.

Wedging Boards

I made a wedging board according to the directions in a ceramic book and it has worked very well up until re-

cently. Lately I have noticed that small bits of plaster are breaking loose and becoming mixed in the clay as I wedge. Before I pour a new bed of plaster, can you suggest any helpful hints on how I can avoid having this happen again?

The trouble could have been caused by using the wrong grade of plaster, by having a poor mixture of plaster and water, or by pouring too shallow a bed of plaster. Potter's plaster should be used for a wedging board, as it should for almost all the ceramist's uses. Plaster should be mixed with water in a ratio of about two pounds of plaster to one quart of water. The depth of plaster for a wedging board should be from 3–5 inches, depending on the area and whether or not it is reinforced. Another suggestion that might be of some help in making a new wedging board is to cover the plaster surface with cotton drill or a light canvas material. Soak the material in water for half an hour, then stretch it over the plaster and tack down all sides. As the cloth dries, it will become very taut.

I am planning to build a wedging board. Do you have any information about the proper height for the wedging surface?

Wedging surface height should vary according to the height and build of the potter to allow full use of the muscles while wedging. Pay particular attention to constructing the board sufficiently low to completely utilize the back muscles, which provide a substantial and efficient wedging force. A variation on the conventional, table-type wedging board is one with the surface slightly elevated above the floor for wedging in the kneeling position.

I have stretched canvas on the top of half my wedging board but it needs repair or replacement if used regularly. The plaster half sometimes leaves small pieces of plaster in my clay. Is any other material used for making wedging board tops?

Concrete makes a good surface that clay won't easily stick to, even after a long period of wedging. It's durable and, if smooth, can be easily cleaned.

Drying Bats

Is there any way you can suggest to speed up the drying of clay slip in large plaster drying bats? I am not trying to dry out the clay completely, but rather to take it from the slip stage to the plastic stage, ready for handbuilding and throwing. I do allow the plaster to dry out between batches of slip, but I don't know of any other short cuts that will help.

Try keeping the plaster molds elevated above the floor—perhaps on wooden forms or even bricks. This allows moisture absorbed from the slip additional surface through which to evaporate more readily.

I have several large plaster slabs which I use for drying out wet clay. These bats worked very well in absorbing excess moisture when they were new, but now I note they are much less effective. Does plaster "wear out" or is there some way I can restore the plaster to its original usefulness?

The absorbency of plaster is affected by the clay, which deposits a film of soluble substances on the porous surface. Even repeated washing with water will not remove this film. The only way in which the plaster can be restored to usefulness is by scraping the surface.

I have been mixing my own clay and never seem to have enough plaster bats on hand for drying out the excess water in the slip. Do you have any suggestions on how this can be done without involving the use of any more plaster bats?

You might try using a thick stack of newspapers as a drying bat. Just pour the clay slip on a 1-inch thick pile of discarded newspapers; this will absorb excess water about as well as plaster does. In addition, a newspaper bat is disposable.

Tools

What can you tell me about elephant ear sponges? I suppose they get their name from their shape, but where are these found, and why do they cost so much?

As far as we know, the sponges are so named because their shape resembles an elephant's ear. The sponges come from the Mediterranean—more specifically, from the waters around Greece. These sponges are found in very deep water—one of the reasons for their higher cost. Formerly there was a similar sponge available from the Philippine waters but these grounds were destroyed in the fighting during World War II.

How can I clean dried latex resist out of my Japanese brushes?

Rubber cement thinner or solvent should work in cleaning your brushes. If they are very caked, you may have to soak the brushes for some time until the resist has been dissolved. To keep the bristles from deforming during soaking, do not allow the weight of the brush to rest on them. Instead, suspend the brush in the container of solvent so that the bristles are immersed but not touching the bottom.

How about a source for good wedging wire? I've used the G string of a guitar for years, but they do break.

Almost any wire will break, usually from too much tension. Among the materials available and useful for the purpose, we find that most potters prefer "piano" wire, although quite a few use stove-pipe wire and recommend it highly.

We have been discussing appropriate names for various ceramic throwing tools, and wondered if there is an accepted name for the sticklike tool which is used to expand the belly of a bottle when the hand can no longer reach inside a constricted neck.

The tool you mention is sometimes called a "bottle stick," or a "throwing stick." Perhaps you would prefer to use the Japanese name which is "egote."

I am familiar with the silicon carbide blades used for cutting bricks, but are there any saw blades available for cutting ceramic tiles with a saber saw?

Remington Arms Company produces "Grit Edge" saw blades which will even make plunge cuts in ceramic tile. Toothless, the blade is coated with tungsten carbide granules, and is also available in a rod-shaped blade which fits a typical hacksaw. Consult your local hardware store for additional information.

Molds

I recently ordered some mold soap, and when it arrived, found to my dismay that it was not a liquid but a paste. Can you give any instructions on how to use it?

Mold soap in the paste form can be made into a liquid by combining one part of the paste with six parts of water (use hot water for best results). Simmer this on the stove until the mixture reaches the consistency of syrup. To use the soap, dip a dampened soft sponge into the liquid and work this up to a lather in a small bowl. It may be necessary to add a few drops of water. Apply this lather generously to the mold surface and wipe away any excess. Three coats are usually required.

Can plaster molds be repaired? I broke a large chunk from the outside of one of my molds and would like to rebuild this section if it can be done successfully.

Adding new plaster to old is not generally recommended. However, if you do wish to attempt it, follow a few simple rules: First, thoroughly roughen or "score" the broken surface deeply in order to give the new plaster a good place to grip. Second, soak the old plaster thoroughly with water so that this area will not draw too much water from the new plaster when it is added. This might cause the added plaster to set too hard and not hold.

Recently I made some simple drape molds from pottery plaster. When the molds were removed, the plaster surfaces were pitted with small holes. Can you provide suggestions for avoiding this defect in the next batch of plaster?

The holes are air bubbles and these should be removed from the plaster when it is mixed, if at all possible. As soon as the plaster has slaked down into the water, stir the mixture gently from the bottom with your hand to force the bubbles to the top. Be careful not to whip the mixture, which would only serve to incorporate more air. When the plaster begins to thicken, and just before pouring the mold, scoop any bubbles from the surface.

I have difficulty with press molds. I make the original models of clay and pour plaster over them to form the molds. The insides of the molds, however, are never as good as the original models; they are wavy and generally imperfect. Is there something incorrect about my procedure?

You may be pouring the plaster too late—the plaster may be too stiff to flow easily and fill all crevices. Another difficulty may be with the original models. Usually, more perfect models can be made by carving them in plaster rather than forming them from clay. The plaster models can be painted with shellac to preserve them and then covered with mold soap to allow the plaster mold to release easily.

I have been searching for information about constructing a plaster mold to use in a hydraulic press for production of stoneware casseroles. Would you know how the compressed air is fed into the mold to release clay from the male and female parts? What type of plaster is used? Is any special preparation necessary?

Production molds for hydraulic pressing are fitted with porous cloth tubing cast into the plaster below the surface. Release of the clay piece occurs when air is forced into the tube and through the porous plaster. A variety of plaster types are used, with the only factors being sufficient porosity and intended life (number of impressions) expected. Hydrocal is common as are a number of even harder plasters. Clay for press molding is generally a bit stiffer than that used for throwing, more of a typical handbuilding consistency or even slightly drier. Clay with less plasticity may be employed in press molding, thus reducing losses through excessive shrinkage and the accompanying cracking.

I am a production potter with an interest in producing drape-molded square slab plates, and am looking for some ideas on materials other than clay for designing the originals. Do you have any suggestions?

It is common practice for studio potters to design drape or press molds for square, slab plates using materials other than clay as the "positive master." Perhaps the most common of these is the wood original—produced with the most versatility by assembling plywood or other board cut with a radial arm saw. Sometimes the press mold itself is made from wood produced in this manner—a very efficient technique with traditional roots.

But for those without woodworking equipment, an extremely simple method of design for slab work is a model cut from cardboard or mattboard with an X-acto knife and steel straight edge, then taped together. A variety of models may be constructed and the best shapes selected for casting. The form is coated with a separator such as hot Vaseline, motor oil or mold soap, then lightly splattered with a thin coating of fine plaster containing a bit of permanent blue ink. Keep this first coat extremely thin, as it will indicate damage to the surface of the mold during both mold making and later production by showing the white plaster beneath it. The blue plaster coat is followed by strips of gauze or cloth soaked in plaster, and thereafter by a thick coating of plaster built up to the desired thickness of from 2–3 inches for a standard plate mold.

Ceramics Monthly published information on various plasters and plaster working techniques in the article "Plaster—The Material," which appeared in the December 1973 issue.

Is it possible and/or advisable to use a bisqued object as a model for a plaster mold? If so, what is the best separator to use and how should it be applied? Can the separator later be removed from the bisque model so that it might be glazed and fired?

It is possible to use a bisque piece as a model for a mold. Mold soap, the usual separator, is not recommended, however; instead, use several coats of lacquer, brushed on and dried between coats. The separator can be removed later by refiring the model to the regular bisque temperature.

Plaster

I have had some plaster for three years, kept in a tightly closed bag. Over this time I have used it with successful results. However, the last time I made a mold, the plaster began setting up immediately, yet failed to harden. Thinking the wrong proportions of plaster and water were mixed, I repeated the process, but again experienced the same results. Can you tell me what is wrong?

Most likely your plaster has begun recrystallization by absorbing moisture from the air, and is no longer usable. Three years is sufficient time for this to happen, even in a tightly closed bag. Fresh plaster in good condition should give three to six minutes pouring time (measured from the commencement of stirring until the mixture begins to set), while old plaster which has had time to absorb moisture from the air may give only one minute. Though it may be possible to calcine recrystallized plaster by heating it to 248°F (120°C), this is not usually practical.

Is patching plaster or builder's plaster a satisfactory material for making molds?

Builder's plaster gives hard and soft spots and it should not be used for mold work. Instead use pottery plaster, which is made especially for ceramic molds and gives the best results. This is fine grained and free from impurities; it gives consistently good molds.

Is there a rule for mixing plaster and water for any given size in making a mold? Using the "hit and miss" method, I usually end up with either more or less than I need.

Figure the size of the mold you want to make in cubic inches (width × length × height), then divide the resultant number by 80. The answer will show the amount of water needed in quarts. To 1 quart of water add 2 pounds, 12 ounces of pottery plaster.

Is there any way to slow down the setting action of plaster so that a person has more time to work with it when making a hump mold? I like to build up the plaster by hand over the clay model without the use of retaining walls, but find the plaster sets up too quickly.

There is a technique called the "slow mix" method

which holds the plaster at the fluid stage for a longer time. After adding the plaster to the water in the correct proportions, allow this to stand for a period of about three minutes without any stirring. After this time, "sweep" the materials together thoroughly, but only until all free water is absorbed into the mix. Then stir the mix for a very short time about every 30 seconds or so, but do not stir continuously, until the proper consistency is reached.

Another method of retarding the setting action is to add sodium citrate (approximately 1–2%) to the plaster mix.

KILNS

Fossil-Fueled Kilns

Recently I came across the terms "periodic" and "continuous" in reference to kilns. Could you explain these?

A "periodic" kiln is one which goes through a cycle of loading, heating, cooling and unloading. Hobby and studio kilns belong in this category. The "continuous" kiln usually is built in a tunnel form, with a hot zone near its center. The ceramic ware moves slowly through the tunnel on cars, from cool area to hot and to cool again. This type of kiln generally is used for industrial operations.

I have decided to build my own gas kiln, but have very little experience in this area. My current residence is in an urban location. Do you have any advice?

For information about building a gas kiln, it would be a good idea to contact another potter in your area who has successfully completed one. This resource person would be invaluable, because the most difficult parts of such an undertaking are to meet local regulations, select and arrange for fuel, decide on the best site, compute a reasonable size and style of kiln, and avoid potential fire hazards. There is a text available which will offer additional help and information: *The Kiln Book*, by Frederick L. Olsen.

I am corresponding with a potter in Bolivia who is trying to establish a pottery but is having trouble firing with propane at 13,000 feet above sea level. Do you have any data for firing at high altitudes?

The higher the elevation the less oxygen is available per cubic foot of air, so the air-to-gas ratio must be increased to compensate. Kilns for high-altitude firing should be designed according to normal principles, then the chimney diameter and the inlet and exit flues should be increased by approximately 50%, and the chimney height increased by 30% to accommodate the larger volume of air required. In *The Kiln Book*, Fred Olsen recommends that the burner orifice be reduced one size for every increment of 2000 feet above 5000 feet altitude; at 13,000 feet the burner orifice should be four sizes smaller than at normal altitudes.

I want to build a kiln wall with hard firebrick inside, a cavity of insulation next, and red facing brick as the outside wall. Can vermiculite be used to fill the cavity, or should it be mixed with something?

Some potters do use vermiculite "as is" to fill an insulating cavity; however, there are two problems with that method. Vermiculite tends to settle over a period of time, leaving the upper portion of the cavity without insulation. Also, vermiculite does not provide any support between the two walls that encase it, so ironwork on the outside of the kiln does not prevent shifting of the inside wall around the firing chamber. An easy solution to both of these problems is to mix the vermiculite with a thick fireclay slip, and pour this into the cavity. There may be some shrinkage when this mass dries and hardens, but you can solve this by adding more, until the cavity is completely filled and the insulation is dry. When mixing the materials, there is no need to measure—simply mix as much vermiculite into the wet slip as you can. The arch may be insulated with loose vermiculite if the weight of the insulation is a problem.

I want to build a 40-cubic-foot downdraft gas kiln, but am limited to a chimney height of no more than 8 feet (the ceiling height is 12 feet). I have read that the stack must

be much higher than this to achieve adequate draft. What can be done?

Using forced air (natural gas or propane) burners, adequate draft can be generated in a 40-cubic-foot, downdraft kiln, even with an 8-foot stack. The best burners for this purpose are those with regulated secondary air which fire through a burner block; that is, a refractory flared burner tube mounted as if it were one of the bricks in the kiln wall. A hood with exhaust fan may be mounted over the short stack if needed to remove exhaust gases.

We have been building a catenary arch kiln of castable refractory, and want to know if there is a rough formula for calculating the amount of castable used.

The volume of castable used in the arch itself can be roughly calculated by running a flexible rule over the arch form, noting this length, and multiplying it times the depth of the arch, times the thickness of castable proposed. Add to this the volume of both end walls, each calculated at ¾ of the height, times the width, times the castable thickness. If the floor, too, is castable, add it to the final volume: multiply its length, width and the proposed castable thickness.

We have been using a silicon carbide shelf as the damper on our downdraft kiln. Periodically this damper breaks and I would like to know if there are any alternatives, other than the common substitutions of stainless steel plate, a mullite shelf or Fiberfrax?

The passive damper is one no-cost alternative: An opening is cut at the back bottom of the chimney; the size of the void should be equivalent to or greater than the area of the chimney diameter. During firing, the chimney draws from both the kiln chamber and through the passive damper opening. The "damper" is regulated by loosely filling the opening with bricks. When completely full, the kiln responds as if an actual damper were completely withdrawn from the flue; when no bricks are in the opening, the kiln responds as if the damper were nearly closed; partial bricking is equivalent to partial dampering. At shutoff, bricks may be pushed clear through to seal the kiln completely from the chimney. The passive damper is amazingly sensitive, and even provides an additional informative view from behind the kiln.

I have a rather well insulated, 24-cubic-foot, softbrick kiln, and the door is bricked by hand each time I fire. When the kiln reaches color, you can see right through the cracks between these bricks, so I would like to find a reasonable way to prevent this energy loss which I believe makes the front of the kiln slightly cooler than the back, and even affects reduction in the front of the ware chamber. Any suggestions?

It is traditional among folk potters in many parts of the world that after the door is bricked, seams are filled, and the door pasted over with very soft, sandy clay in order to prevent needless heat loss and maintain a desired atmosphere in the ware chamber. With insulating firebrick, however, this method is not very practical, because the bricks are relatively susceptible to abrasion and breakage—characteristics which make them rather poor for a slurry-sealed door, and in fact rather poor for a bricked-up door. Instead of a hand-bricked door, consider substituting a large sheet of steel with handles screwed or welded to the back, and sufficient layers of refractory fiber felt "wallpapered" on the steel to protect it. This fiber door would not over insulate, even in a hardbrick kiln, but rather would save much fuel and possibly prevent a few back problems as well.

Electric Kilns

I got an old electric kiln at a garage sale. It works, but I am wondering how high it can be safely fired. Is there some sort of test that would indicate this?

According to Harrop Industries, if the elements in your kiln will attract a magnet, this indicates they are Kanthal wire and, therefore, may be fired to Cone 10.

All of my clays, glazes and various firing techniques are keyed to my 7-cubic-foot electric kiln. I am very much interested in a small kiln for firing test samples and small objects when I cannot wait for a full kiln load. I'm told, however, that the "test kiln" would give me quite differ-

ent results from my larger kiln because it fires so quickly. Can you offer some comments?

The problem may not be as acute as your advisors make it. Although there would no doubt be differences in some results, in many cases there would not be any noticeable difference. The very small test kiln is becoming more and more popular because it can give glaze test results so quickly and because it is so handy for firing small pieces.

For our school I recently bought a new electric kiln which does a fine job bisque firing ware, but will not fire to the maximum stoneware temperature listed on the kiln. I've checked the elements—they all glow appropriately when the kiln is on its "high" setting, but the kiln still doesn't make temperature. And it's not a cheap brand, either. Do some manufacturers make their kilns underpowered, or what's the problem?

All manufactured electric kilns (if in proper condition) are designed to fire to their specified cone range even with a densely packed load. When problems like this occur in a new kiln there is generally another cause. According to a representative of A.R.T. Studio Clay Company, "The normal household current is 220/240 volts. It is written 220/240 because of normal fluctuations during the day. For example, at noon on a hot summer day when everyone is using their air conditioners the voltage may be as low as 220 volts, and in the dead of night when most appliances are off, it may be as high as 240 volts. If your kiln needs 230 volts to operate at peak efficiency you may have trouble reaching maximum cones when the voltage drops to 220 volts. In some areas, primarily industrial or institutional, it is not uncommon to find 208/230 volts since it is more economical to operate and most appliances and motors are not affected by the slightly lower voltage. But if the kiln is rated for 230 volts it may not reach temperature, especially in the upper ranges.

"Therefore, it is of critical importance that the correct voltage be determined and the proper voltage specified when ordering a kiln.

"A 220/240-volt kiln hooked up to a 208/230-volt

service will low fire satisfactorily but will not reach maximum temperatures efficiently, if at all.

"A 208/230-volt kiln hooked up to 220/240-volt service will put undue strain on the elements and switches, and in some instances, will burn them out very quickly."

I have a fairly small electric kiln that used to fire to Cone 1. I rewired it with different elements and altered the electrical power to fire to Cone 10. Now I have a very high breakage rate during these high-temperature firings. The kiln was originally rated at 110 volts and had two on-and-off switches. It is now wired for 220 volts and uses one switch. Is all the pottery breaking because of the small area heating up so quickly? If so, can you suggest some ways of slowing down the rate of temperature increase?

It is not advisable to rewire electric kilns except as intended by the manufacturer. It is possible to do so with success, or even to build an electric kiln, provided you have control over other variables, such as element resistance, chamber size, composition of the refractory materials, insulation characteristics, and the electrical control equipment. In addition to control of these variables, you should have a strong knowledge of electricity and its application to kilns before attempting any adjustments. In most cases, you will find that the kiln has been engineered for its best performance as originally produced by the manufacturer.

Although your clay body could be at fault (and there are many bodies which will take an extremely fast temperature rise like the raku bodies), it is more likely that your problem is the result of increasing the electrical power input without adapting other variables in your kiln's construction. One possible solution would be to install an industrial rheostat to provide complete control over the temperature regulation of your kiln. The drawback to this suggestion is that such equipment, if purchased new, may cost hundreds of dollars. In most cases it would be less expensive to buy a new kiln unless you can find suitable electrical controls in a surplus or electrical component store.

Another alternative is to increase the size of the firing chamber with additional firebrick. If you are fortunate, the kiln may fire evenly, and you will find that a significantly larger firing chamber will reduce the speed of temperature climb. But, this will also lower the maximum firing temperature of the kiln. Kiln manufacturers are best acquainted with the characteristics of their product. Consult with them before changing any part of your electric kiln.

Will firing ash glazes in an electric kiln do any harm to the electric elements?

Ash glazes will not harm your electric kiln heating elements, and there are many fine ash glaze formulas that can be experimentally developed by the potter. Oxidation-fired ash glazes generally give reduction-like effects that seem to be much sought by those without access to a fuel-burning kiln. The mottled surface characteristic of the typical ash glaze can be quite handsome on both functional and decorative ceramics. *Ceramics Monthly* has published several articles that might be of interest to you: "Wood Ash Glazes for Cone 8," September 1980; "Vine Ash Glazes," May 1981; "Wood-Ash Glazes in Oxidation," January 1983; "Slip-Ash Glazes," November 1984; and "A Rational View of Wood Ash," December 1985.

Will the use of alkaline carbonates as described by Richard Behrens in "An Alternative to Salt Glazing" (October 1974 *Ceramics Monthly*) have a deleterious effect on an electric kiln?

Vapor glazing, regardless of which compound is used, will cause deterioration of heating elements and soft firebrick in an electric kiln.

My electric kiln is rated for firing to 2300°F (Cone 8). But a recent load accidentally overfired to Cone 10 with no apparent harm to the kiln. Is it possible to continue firing at Cone 10 in a kiln rated for Cone 8 maximum firing temperature?

Ceramics Monthly recently discussed this problem with a leading kiln manufacturer who commented that kilns produced from first quality insulating refractories and elements should be able to fire to Cone

10, but with much more cracking of brick, increased element wear, and more thermocouple corrosion. Because kiln producers have various warranty requirements, manufacturing techniques, and use various grades of material, ceramists should contact their manufacturer for information on overfiring.

From time to time cracks appear between the brick in my electric kiln. I have mended them with various materials; but after several firings, the mended places will crack again. Can you suggest a more permanent way to make such repairs?

Fine cracks often show up in the light-weight insulating brick used in electric kilns. Generally it's to be expected, because of thermal shock of the fast heating and cooling. Where actual pieces of the brick do not fall out, cracks are best left without cement. The very porous nature of insulating brick makes it difficult for the cement to hold even during drying.

It's evident that the cements you have used lack the proper bond after firing. Most electric kiln manufacturers and refractory brick manufacturers can provide you with the suitable cement. When a cement is to be applied, wet the surface to be repaired, make a thick paste of the cement with water, trowel it onto both edges and hold the pieces in place until set. After about 24 hours of drying, the kiln may be fired. The cement will become hard and should stay in place.

Burners

We have had to reduce the size of burner ports on our 27-cubic-foot downdraft kiln in order to get a reduction atmosphere, but this causes thermocouples to burn off our Big Bertha burners. I've written to a manufacturer, and they suggest not reducing the port size. Any other ideas?

It would help to know the current size of your burner ports to make sure they are not excessive, but barring that, there are a number of steps you can take to improve reduction. The first is to check the rest of the kiln for air leaks, filling them with commercial refractory cement or homemade fireclay mortar. Your kiln may have a door which is bricked in before each firing, and air leaks through these unmortared bricks are a common cause of poor reduction. A simple solution to the door problem is to lay the inside courses of the door in the normal manner, but begin the outside bricking with a row of "splits" to offset horizontal seams. Once or twice, though, as the door is built up, splits should be added so that a level tie course can be laid for a more stable door.

Another simple solution to your thermocouple problem is to see if the burners will stay ignited with the thermocouple rotated to the bottom of the burner. More importantly, consider pulling the burners back from the ports as far as they will fire efficiently. If these precautions are insufficient, you might consider borrowing a gas analyzer (a number of potters use them for reduction firing) to determine the precise burner port size for adequate reduction throughout your kiln.

If that is still insufficient, thermocouples placed on pilot burners are a preferred alternative, and your burners might be adapted in this manner so that the thermocouple is not exposed to the concentration of heat it receives when placed in the direct path of the main burner. *Ceramics Monthly* published an article on making pilot burners in the September 1978 issue, and just in case you don't have that one, xerographic reprints of CM articles are available from Xerox University Microfilms, Serials Bid Coordinator, 300 North Zeeb Road, Ann Arbor, Michigan 48106.

The cost of thermocouples has risen so high that I would like to find out if a broken unit can be resoldered, and if so, to have instructions as to the method, and types of solder used.

Ceramics Monthly contacted a representative of A. Cottone Instruments, Inc., who provided the following information: Thermocouple repairs are effected by arc welding the tip rather than soldering. Generally, such repairs are not considered practical, since the reconnection does not last significantly. Ceramists commonly use one of two types of thermocouples. The chromel/alumel "Type K" is a low-cost product which is best replaced rather than repaired, because rewelding may result in inaccurate calibration of the instrument. A platinum thermocouple may be reasonably repaired in limited cases.

I am building an 18-cubic-foot stoneware kiln which should fire to Cone 10. I have read three different sources that offer widely different opinions about the amount of heat needed to fire each cubic foot of kiln space. These estimates range from 6000 to 30,000 Btu's per cubic foot. I have ordered four burners at 35,000 Btu's each. Will this be sufficient, or should I be guided by the higher estimates?

The number of Btu's needed to heat a cubic foot of your kiln depends on the amount of insulation the kiln provides, as well as the actual Btu's you get from each burner (which depends on the regulation of primary and secondary air), the chimney characteristics, the tightness of the kiln door, length of the path the flame must take through the kiln, and many other factors. Because of these variables, it is suggested that you follow the higher figures for Btu's per cubic foot of kiln space. It is much better to have an over-powered kiln than to have one that will not reach the desired temperatures. Any extra Btu's will be useful on days when the gas pressure drops from a change in the barometric pressure, or on particularly stubborn firings due to stacking, or when something falls over in the kiln blocking a burner, etc. If you are buying manufactured burners, you will find many firms pleased to help you determine your needs, provided you can give them complete information about your kiln's design, composition and proposed fuel.

Fuels

I am considering construction of a new kiln and am wondering if you could provide comparative statistics on the Btu's available in natural gas, fuel oil and electricity.

An average rating for the fuels you mentioned is:

1 cubic foot of natural gas = 1000 Btu's

1 gallon of No. 2 fuel oil = 140,000 Btu's

1 kilowatt of electricity = 3400 Btu's

Another way to look at this is that 41 kilowatts of electricity are equal to 1 gallon of No. 2 fuel oil, which is equal to 140 cubic feet of natural gas (assuming efficient combustion). By the way, a Btu is defined as the amount of heat required to raise the temperature of 1 pound of water 1°F. In more imaginable terms, it is approximately the heat found in one standard wooden match.

We are wondering if there is a way to prevent rust associated with the use of water in a manometer which reads gas pressure on our kiln.

Add a bit of potassium permanganate to the water. This compound will not affect the manometer reading, and will help stop rust in the associated fittings.

What can be done to remedy fuel freeze-up? I use a 173-gallon propane tank with a high-pressure regulator (0–15 pounds) that feeds a 1-inch gas line to my 16-cubic-foot kiln. Normally, I fire at 2 pounds of pressure for 8 hours to reach Cone 6. In cold weather the regulator freezes up and the pressure drops significantly even when the tank is more than half full. What do you suggest?

To understand the cause and remedies for your fuel line/regulator freeze-up you should understand how gas pressure, volume and temperature relate to each other during firing, as expressed by the following mathematical statement: PV/T. When firing your kiln, both pressure and volume are reduced, thus directly reducing tank and fuel line temperature in proportion to the volume and speed of gas flow. When the outside temperature is low the problem is complicated further.

We recommend the better (two-stage) propane system discussed in "Low-Pressure Propane Firing" by John Perri in the December 1976 *Ceramics Monthly*. This should solve your problem outright. If that kind of adaption is too extensive, here are some general comments about propane firing and alternative courses of action:

Make sure you begin each firing with a full tank. If that is insufficient, a larger regulator, larger pipe and fittings may solve the problem by giving the propane more volume to flow through. Try to locate the source of freeze-up, and give the fuel more room there. If the problem is still unsolved, acquiring a larger propane tank is the next course of action, since this offers a greater propane volume from which to draw.

Some potters go to great lengths to work with the system at hand, sometimes placing an electric blanket over the propane tank, using heat lamps, etc. Such "make-do" techniques are ill advised because of the obvious hazards they pose.

Refractories

I have access to a large quantity of used firebrick at a very inexpensive price. All that is known about this brick is that it has "Ranger" stamped on it, and that it came out of a smelter in southern Oklahoma. I have fired one of these seven times to Cone 10 in a salt kiln and it seems to be fine, but what will happen with a ton of weight on top of it? How does one find the temperature and source of a brick such as this?

The bricks you are interested in were made by General Refractories Company in Texas, and are rated for high-heat duty. You can find the producer for most brick brands by consulting a copy of the *Products Directory of the Refractories Institute* (301 Fifth Avenue, Pittsburgh, Pennsylvania 15222) available through your local library using its interlibrary loan program. This reference is also commonly found in ceramic engineering departments across the U.S. When buying used brick, the real question is how used?

Typically when bricks age with heat exposure they become more brittle, more inclined to spall and crack, but these conditions can be determined by a physical inspection including striking sample bricks against one another to make a condition determination. Most of the time, used brick is a great bargain for the potter, and can be employed with only slightly less kiln life. And there is now a diminishing chance of obtaining the inferior low- and medium-heat-duty bricks, as few are made any more—industry trends point to the production of high-heat-duty bricks only in future years.

I recently moved to Maine and am having trouble locating special firebrick shapes. I therefore am looking for a source of castable refractory materials in the New England area. Can you help?

Although castable refractory is available from a number of commercial sources, you might try making your own. You will save considerable money, and all the materials should be available from any ceramic supply company and your local building supply store. Get the portland cement, vermiculite and sawdust from the building supply; the fireclay from either source; and the rest of the materials from the ceramic supply company. The following castable refractory recipe should be mixed with water and rammed into forms in the usual manner. The second formula is for a castable insulation which may be mixed with water and applied to the outside of the castable refractory without ramming, and will provide added insulation if needed. Both recipes list ingredients by volume for ease of preparation. Use any container and count its volume as one part.

Castable Refractory for Kiln Construction

Portland Cement 2	parts by volume
Alumina Hydrate 1	
Pea Grog 4	
Fireclay 4	
Sawdust...2	
Vermiculite 3	
16	parts by volume

A self-hardening refractory suitable for stoneware and porcelain firing temperatures.

Kiln Insulation

Portland Cement 2	parts by volume
Kentucky Ball Clay (OM 4) 2	
Fireclay 4	
Sawdust...2	
Vermiculite 3	
13	parts by volume

A self-hardening, applied kiln insulation suitable for stoneware and porcelain temperatures.

I want to make my own kiln furniture and am wondering if you could provide a recipe for making shelves.

A recipe advocated by the English potter Harry Davis is a mixture of 50% fireclay with 50% grog, the latter being refired to increase its mullite content.

I would like to make my own stilts like the three-pointed ones sold at ceramics suppliers. What are they made of?

The following recipe should provide high-quality stilts when the forms are press molded and bisque fired in the stoneware range:

Stilt Body

Ball Clay	78 %
Georgia Kaolin (ASP 400)	10
Flint	12
	100 %

I am interested in making insulating firebrick for use in kilnbuilding. Can you give some information on how this is accomplished?

Most ceramists who have attempted insulating brick fabrication will agree that the effort and materials cost hardly justify home production. Portland cement-based castable materials are considered a better solution to inexpensive kilnbuilding. But on an experimental basis, insulating firebrick may be made by mixing with a thick fireclay slip any materials which will leave an assortment of closely spaced air pockets after firing. Examples include combustible materials such as sawdust and wood shavings, and expanded minerals such as perlite—a natural volcanic glass. The fireclay mixture is then placed in brick molds, extruded, sliced or rammed into the required shapes.

Kiln Shelves

I use a silicon carbide shelf as a floor in my gas-fired raku kiln, but wonder if there is some other material which is less expensive as a substitute?

Standard perforated house bricks are excellent for raku kiln floors. When supported above the firebox, the holes allow flame to pass through to the bottom of the firebox. The low-fire house brick floor is easily replaced when deteriorated, but because of its thickness it is structurally sound for many firings. When replacement bricks are needed, new ones may be purchased from any building supply company.

How does one completely clean kiln shelves where the wash is adhered with glaze fumes from electric firing? The wash won't totally come off even by scraping my clay shelves.

Since most kiln wash contains a substantial amount of free silica, it is important that the potter minimize exposure to dust from wash removal. Because of this, the lower velocity methods (scraping by hand as opposed to using power tools) are preferred in combination with wearing a NIOSH-approved dust mask. Begin with a very coarse file followed by grinding with a hand-held piece of broken silicon carbide kiln shelf, or even a piece of hard firebrick to finish.

Many potters today are avoiding kiln wash entirely, firing questionable glazed ware on a setter tile (a small slab under the foot or base of the work matching its composition and state—either green or bisqued). The advantage of this method is that shelves may be repeatedly fired inverted from the previous firing, thereby eliminating warpage and greatly extending the useful life of a shelf. This applies not only to clay shelves but also to silicon carbide, even when fired in a salt kiln.

Kiln shelves may also be professionally sandblasted.

We've been having a discouraging and expensively bad time with warping kiln shelves which leave our oxidation-fired pots with rocking bases. We noted the comment about not using kiln wash and inverting the shelves after each firing, but the clay we use will fuse to the shelf without a kiln wash barrier, and it's unrealistic to make separate setter tiles for each piece. What can you suggest?

By dusting the shelves with alumina before setting ware you could avoid having to use kiln wash and at the same time keep pots from sticking to the shelves. The alumina dusts easily away and may be reused firing after firing. Another solution is to mix alumina with wax resist and coat the bottom of each object; the wax burns away, leaving a light film of alumina, which may be washed or dusted away after firing.

I have been using 18×18×⅝-inch silicon carbide kiln shelves for Cone 10, but find that after firing three or four loads of ware the shelves develop hairline cracks. The defect starts at one edge, gradually lengthening toward the center of the shelf, and widening with each firing. Mullite shelves used in the same kiln do not crack at all. Can you explain the cause of this problem and suggest good replacement shelves?

There is a significant problem which is common with square, or nearly square shelves—the nature of silicon carbide is to grow equally in all directions as it is fired, and this would cause a square or nearly square shelf to have a tendency to pull itself apart. If the potter substitutes two 9×18×⅝-, or 9×18×¾-inch shelves, this should help.

Many ceramists are unaware that there are several formulas used in the manufacture of silicon carbide shelves. An average potter's periodic kiln would need an entirely different shelf composition than would industry using a car or shuttle kiln. The formula would be changed again for a fast-firing cycle.

Hairline cracks may also be caused by cold air striking the silicon carbide, resulting in thermal shock to the shelf. To avoid this, peepholes and the door should be tightly closed during temperature rise, and all kiln openings should be shut tightly throughout cooling. The door should not be opened when kiln temperature is above 450°F.

Mullite shelves, because of their considerably different composition, are affected quite differently by kiln conditions. But, silicon carbide shelves continue to be the longest wearing, and most trouble free for both industrial and studio use.

The shelves from my reduction kiln also fit my new electric kiln. But I remember hearing something about silicon carbide shelves not being good for oxidation firing. Is that correct? If I could use these shelves in both kilns, that would save quite a bit.

Silicon carbide shelves are not recommended for

oxidation firing. Though the material offers high strength and resistance to abrasion and (in most instances) to thermal shock, it is a conductor of electricity, and therefore might pose a hazard. Additionally, silicon carbide, especially the oxide-bonded group, has a poor resistance to oxidation. In an oxidizing atmosphere, SiO_2 is formed within the shelf, causing an increase in volume. Normally this oxidation reaction is not uniform, resulting in shelf distortion. Most manufacturers recommend mullite or clay shelves for electric kilns.

Is there some way to differentiate between a surface fracture and a crack which goes clear through a section of kiln shelf?

The extent of kiln shelf fracture may be simply determined by sprinkling dry alumina on the shelf, balancing it on a centrally located post, and tapping the shelf sharply. Wherever a crack goes through the kiln shelf, the two halves of the shelf act as a tuning fork, vibrating at different rates and causing alumina to part at the crack.

How hot are silicon carbide shelves fired?

From 3236° to 3992°F.

My kiln shelves are old and have had much hard use, but I think there is a lot of life still left in them. However, so much glaze has dripped down and adhered to the shelves (in spite of coatings of kiln wash), that they are quite uneven and sometimes it is difficult to set ware on them. Is there any way to level these shelves?

Try adding a fair amount of grog to your kiln wash the next time you coat the shelves. By applying this mixture quite heavily, you should be able to produce a level kiln wash surface.

Kiln Wash

I've been using the typical kiln wash of 50% kaolin and 50% flint, but because of concern about breathing free silica unnecessarily, I am wondering if you can recommend a kiln wash without free silica hazards.

Many potters have switched to a kiln wash of 50% any kaolin and 50% alumina hydrate for the health reasons you mention. This wash contains no free silica, and has application in all ceramic atmospheres, including salt glazing.

I have been making my own kiln wash from equal parts by weight of kaolin and silica. Why does this crack and sometimes flake off? I am firing at Cone 04 and Cone 6.

In all probability you are coating your shelves too heavily with the wash. Some potters dampen their kiln shelves slightly before applying the wash, in order to avoid too heavy of a buildup. Of course, extra drying time must be allowed when this practice is followed. Temperature is not a factor in your case, since both materials are refractory enough to withstand the temperatures you are reaching. Some potters scrape off the old kiln wash after every firing, and apply fresh each time; others simply will patch up any bare spots on the shelves until the surface becomes too uneven for proper stacking.

WARE

History

I noted with interest comments concerning a Bellarmine jug, and how the gray beard form caricatured Cardinal Bellarmine, a 17th-century Italian prelate. Why did potters select him for caricature?

Bellarmine jugs represent a very early form of potters' activism as the caricature is said to have resulted because of Bellarmine's persecution of Reformed Protestant potters.

I recently came across an old earthenware butter pot marked with the name of Thomas Daniel. Can you tell me anything about it?

In England, butter pots made for sale to Midland farmers and markets were once suspected of being a means for consumer fraud. During the 17th century both potter and farmer were accused of attempting to mislead the customer: the potter by making pots with extra thick bottoms, which meant less butter was needed to fill them; the farmer by putting poor quality butter under the good quality top layer. To control the potters, a 1662 act of Parliament required that a pot of butter weigh 20 pounds of which the pot was to weigh no more than 6 pounds; furthermore, the pot had to be marked with the name of the potter.

Marked examples indicate Thomas Daniel was one of Burslem's foremost butter pot makers, and documents do record that in 1682 he was accused (with Thomas Cartwright) of monopolizing the trade and doubling prices.

As a functional potter, I am always looking for "new" forms that might add to my current line of kitchen- and tableware. Often I find ideas in antique shops, buy the interesting piece and bring it back to the studio for development into something of my own design. Recently, I found a covered jar that really has me stumped. Inside the lid are horizontal ceramic spikes protruding toward the center. There are two rows of these spikes inside the body of the jar, too, all protruding from the outside wall toward the center like spokes on a wheel, except not touching in the center. Can you tell me what this form is and how it was used?

The form you describe is an egg beater. An egg was broken, then dropped onto the spikes of the jar which, when closed, could be swirled or shaken like a cocktail shaker. The forms were doubtless difficult to clean and easily broken—hence their demise.

I am having considerable difficulty finding information about rice grain porcelain. Any insight you can give on this subject will be appreciated.

Rice grain porcelain is pierced ware in which the cut areas resemble the shape and size of rice grains. The "grains" usually are placed in a geometric or decorative pattern, and filled with translucent glaze. The success of the method depends on the width of the areas to be spanned with glaze, and the viscosity of the recipe used to fill the holes. While the most notable examples are thought to be from China, the Persians imitated the Oriental ware using a soft-paste porcelainlike body, and these pieces are known as Gombroon ware. One source states that this ware dates as early as the 12th century, but it is usually associated with the 17th and 18th. Rice grain ware has been made commercially, especially in Europe, and can be found on the shelves of contemporary gift shops. The rice grain pattern is generally associated with a glazed, true porcelain body, thrown or cast to be somewhat translucent overall, but with greater translucency in the perforations.

I am interested in information about lithophanes. Can you provide some basic data about their production and history?

A lithophane is a thin, translucent porcelain object with images designed in intaglio and illuminated with light transmitted through the clay body. The density and thickness of the body determine the amount of light passing through a specific section of the image. While also known as "Berlin transparencies," lithophanes have appeared throughout Europe as early as the second decade of the 19th century, and most are figurative in design and quite realistic in style.

Originating usually with a wax carving from which a plaster mold is taken, lithophanes may also result from an original plaster or bisque "master" as in the case of those produced by Wedgwood. Finishing techniques for lithophanes span a variety of methods; both glazed and unglazed have been produced. While usually associated with true porcelain, they may be made in other clays, both colored and uncolored, provided that the translucency is sufficient. Lithophanes are usually associated with their application as decorative panels in lampshades.

Can you provide information on Belleek—its body composition, firing temperature, and glazing procedure?

This fine, thin ware with a clear or pale pearlescence was first produced in Ireland near Belfast, and production continues today at that locale. Other ware in the Belleek tradition was made during the 19th century in both England and the United States. Several sources mention the body as being related to Parian, fired to vitrification, but at a lower temperature than true "hard paste" porcelain. The Belleek body, made from a local clay, may have been fluxed with frit, a feldspathic material or barium sulfate. The ware was generally cast, although some was described as being "potted"; Belleek baskets were formed from extruded clay strands woven over plaster forms. Bisque firing occurred at a high temperature in a coal-burning kiln, with glaze, overglaze and luster firings at progressively lower cones. Saggars protected the ware from the kiln atmosphere. Contemporary ceramists may be able to experimentally duplicate Belleek using a Parian body and commercial lusters, fuming or vapor glazing in a saggar. Glaze consultant Richard Behrens provided a recipe for a parian casting slip in the CM handbook, *Glaze Projects*:

Parian Casting Slip (Cone 4)

Nepheline Syenite	600.0	grams
Kentucky Ball Clay (OM 4)	400.0	grams
	1000.0	grams
Add: Water	400.0	milliliters
Soda Ash	0.8	grams
Sodium Silicate	0.8	grams

A glaze to fit this white-firing vitreous body is:

Transparent Glaze (Cone 4)

Lithium Carbonate	9.1 %
Nepheline Syenite	34.6
Whiting	10.9
Kaolin	12.2
Flint	33.2
	100.0 %

This batch should be applied thinly and may be used for glazing the inside of forms for containing liquids.

What is the ceramic process for making "cultured marble"—an imitation of the stone? Is there any significant history of ware made by this process?

"Cultured marble" is made by partially wedging together two (or more) differently colored clays.

Surfaces which have been thrown or excessively worked may require scraping to completely reveal the marbled surface. A similar effect can also be achieved by partially mixing colored slips before casting.

Marbled ware was produced by Wedgwood during the 18th century; however, one source notes that such ware was made in China as early as the Tang dynasty.

FORMING TECHNIQUES

As a beginning potter (two months), I am running into a few problems, most of which should dissolve with experience, I hope. One of the most troublesome seems to come from using too much water when throwing (things collapsing, etc.). Is there any way I can tell how much water to use?

The use of too much water is common for a beginner. Only enough should be used to keep the clay lubricated as you work. Try to discipline yourself by allowing very little water in your container; another suggestion is to use slip instead of water, and still another is to hold a very small dampened sponge as you pull up a pot.

We have been producing teapots, and are now having a problem with spouts appearing somewhat twisted after firing. The flat cut lip is lower on the right side than on the left. Can we add something to the clay to prevent this?

Spouts which seem to twist after firing are the result of a phenomenon called "clay memory." Narrow, thrown spouts are particularly subject to this problem, and potters experiencing it should cut the lip at an angle adjusted for the potential clockwise twist. The spout (as the piece goes into the kiln) should thus be a little bit askew, and on firing will straighten to the appropriate position. The potter Harry Davis used to press mold his spouts to avoid this problem.

Where can I get information about making screw-on caps for my pots?

There are two good sources for this information—*Ceramics Monthly* published an article in the September 1972 issue by Robert F. Eilenberger, titled "Flask with Screw Cap." This article demonstrates a method of making these caps using coils for threads. Another source is Michael Cardew's text, *Pioneer Pottery*. Appendices five and six show the template method of Cipriano Piccolpasso, and the tap-and-die nut method.

Do you have any advice on making press molds from bisque clay rather than plaster?

Bisque will give better wear than will plaster, which is much softer. You may not be able to get as much detail in your clay press mold as you can with plaster, however. If you are going to make clay press molds, remember to account for drying and firing shrinkage.

Can sand be used to make a mold for draping clay shapes?

Sand can be used quite successfully for making a mold for draping or pressing. The shape should be a simple one without complex curves. The sand itself should be a fine beach or lake variety; sand used for concrete is too coarse to hold a shape very well. The sand should be dampened, then packed tightly in a box before the center area is scooped out to make the mold. The clay slab being shaped in the sand mold must be relatively thin and it should be lifted carefully into the mold area and gently shaped. When the clay shape is dry it is lifted out of the improvised mold.

I do a lot of work with children's groups. They always seem to have difficulty rolling out coils for making coil-built pots and animals. Their coils seem to go flat and uneven. Do you have any suggestions to help on this?

The clay you're using may be too stiff for rolling coils easily. Try wedging more water into it to make it more moist. Also, have the children roll out the coils using the palms of their hands as well as their fingers to get a longer rolling action. Additionally, your working surface might be a poor one for this technique. One of the best materials to work on is a sheet of Masonite. It is smooth and yet porous enough to absorb and hold just the right amount of water to make rolling coils easy. Dampen the Masonite with a sponge, then wait until all surface water has disappeared before rolling out the coils.

Extruding

We have been extruding flower vases, then slab rolling bases, but find the process of cutting and adding slab bottoms both time consuming and less than creative. Have you any ideas for a more efficient method that doesn't involve our slab roller which we'd rather use for other production purposes?

There are many solutions to your problem, including cutting an extrusion so that a section of the wall can be flattened to form the bottom, removing the center piece from your extrusion die and wire-cutting bottom slabs of exactly the right diameter, or extruding a ribbon from which bottoms can be cut and applied. But perhaps the most efficient method for adding bottoms to extruded forms is to set the tubes upright on a plaster slab, then pour casting slip (a related recipe) as thick as the desired bottom into the extrusion. The plaster draws out excess water, and the forms can be quickly removed from the plaster bat and set aside with little need for additional finishing. You may have to experiment with various compositions in order to get the shrinkage and water content right for a minimum of cracked pieces, but once these technicalities are worked out for your own clay body, the process is extremely fast.

Jiggering

I wish to build a jiggering machine for making plates part of my studio production. Would the rotation be the same speed as a standard potter's wheel?

Jiggering can be accomplished within the range of the typical potter's wheel rotation although there are advantages to faster speeds, which include better uniformity and economy of production. Industrial jiggering machines rotate at approximately 400 rpm.

Forming and Drying Tile

Can you provide any information on forming tile from clay powder without additions of water?

Dry pressing of ceramic objects was first patented in 1840, and the process (invented by Richard Prosser of Birmingham, England) was first applied to the production of ceramic buttons, and later to tile. Called "dust pressing," the dies were made of metal, and according to the book, *Victorian Ceramic Tiles*, "If the tile had a surface pattern, then a die was placed at the bottom of the mould. This plate or die was set to the correct level, according to the thickness required: for a 6×6×³⁄₈-inch wall tile, just over ⁵⁄₈ inch of dust was put into the mould.

"The presser wiped the plates clean with a greasy rag, filled the mould with dust clay and scraped the surface level. Then he slowly lowered the press by turning the large horizontal wheel at the top which was about 6 feet in diameter. This allowed the air to escape from the clay in the mould. The screw was then lifted slightly and quickly lowered again with a force of about 30 tons vertical pressure to compact and face the tile. It was forced out of the mould by means of a foot-pedal and the operation was quickly repeated..."

Dust pressing is widely applied today in industry, but it has received little use by the potter.

I have problems with tiles warping and cracking (fine cracks from the corners occurring in bisque firing). Are there any special methods for limiting such problems?

Warping and cracking of ceramic tiles are common problems in hand production. These can be minimized by rolling tile slabs in two or three directions, flipping the slab and doing the same from the other side. Slow, even drying, and firing on edge with air space all around the tile will also limit these problems.

I have tried almost every technique but I still have trouble drying large rolled-out tiles without warping. Can you help?

Try using a clay body that has a low drying shrinkage. The less shrinkage, the less warpage. Add a good percentage of grog or other nonplastic material like flint (if the body will permit) to the clay to help cut down on shrinkage.

Dry the piece as slowly and as evenly as possible. Edges will dry before the center, so you may have to cover the edges with damp cloth. Turn the tile frequently so the underside will dry as quickly as the top side, keep the piece in a well-controlled damp box, dry it sandwiched between plaster bats, put weights on it, hollow out or cut ridges on the underside to eliminate some of the bulk, etc.

Allow shrinkage movement during the drying stages by setting the tile on newspaper or cloth. This is important during firing, too, and can be accomplished by setting the tiles on a bed of flint so they can move evenly and easily as they go through their firing shrinkages.

Casting

I am having difficulty casting in a two-piece plate mold. The mold stands vertically; there is a narrow slit leading to the lip of the plate for pouring and emptying. Pieces turn out hollow instead of solid and more often than not the plate pulls apart when the mold is opened. Another difficulty: I have to keep adding slip to the mold as the level goes down and the plate invariably shows streaks even after glazing and firing.

There are so many variables and possible complications in slip casting it is very difficult to correctly diagnose a specific problem by "remote control."

The difficulty can be (and often is) the slip. If it casts properly in other molds, however, this possibility must be eliminated.

The mold design can also be introducing the problem. In general, it is much easier to successfully pour a piece of this type if the mold lies horizontal with the opening through the foot of the plate rather than at the lip. Also, it seems there should be a larger well at the top to hold an excess of slip so that refilling over a long period of time is not necessary. This is mere speculation since we do not know the exact size, shape and dimensions of this particular mold.

Is there any way I can avoid pinholes in my slip-cast pieces?

If the holes appear in the greenware, it may be the result of air being introduced during mixing or pouring of the slip. Follow deairing procedures such as allowing the slip to stand overnight before use, or pounding on the walls of the slip container to loosen any bubbles from the bottom or sides. A bell jar or other vacuum device makes efficiently deaired slip, but such equipment is impractical for most potters who might do occasional casting. When pouring slip, let it flow gently, avoiding splashes that cause air to be trapped.

Pinholes originating after firing may be the result of undissolved crystals of soluble salts reintroduced in the slip in the bodies of cast rejects. The solution is to discard rejected castings, or to mix the slip much longer.

FINISHING

Trimming

I lose many pots each year because often I can't, or forget to, trim them when the moisture level is just right. The ware gets too dry for footing and has to be discarded. Any solutions?

Pots that are too dry for footing need not be discarded, as there are at least two successful rewetting techniques commonly in use. If the ware is completely dry, it should be totally submersed in water for about ten seconds, removed and given a good shake in the same manner as one would shake off excess glaze, then wrapped in plastic sheet for a few hours during which time the water absorption will even out. If the ware is so thick or so completely dry that this proves insufficient, the process can be repeated, or the following technique applied: Pots too dry for footing are placed upright on a wet sheet of newspaper freshly laid in the bottom of an inexpensive Styrofoam picnic cooler. When left overnight, the foot should soften to a perfect consistency for trimming, while the rest of the pot stays hard.

Try both of these techniques, as the humidity in your region (which affects drying time) may affect your evaluation of which is better, or if they should be used in combination.

I notice that some pottery is made with a foot rim and that other pieces do not have any foot treatment at all. Is there any particular reason for even making the foot?

Here is what Carlton Atherton wrote about the foot in an article that appeared in *Ceramics Monthly* in November 1954: "The foot absorbs and distributes mechanical shock, acting as a safeguard against breakage. It can be inverted, in which case it is not apparent but a part of the form. More often it is raised, lifting the body of the vessel from the plane of support to give the eye freer access to the form itself, allowing attention to be given the dominant part of the pot rather than to be led away from it. The type of foot to be used calls for careful selection and its proportions for discreet adjustment. A high, narrow foot gives refinement and elegance, a low foot gives stability and confidence, but extremes in either direction court disaster. A narrow foot imparts lift and buoyancy to the pot but this foot must be broad enough to assure psychological security as well as actual safety from overturning. A broad foot furnishes such assurance, but if extreme, will choke the form and give it an earthbound heaviness."

I have been using a heavily grogged clay which has very good throwing and sculptural qualities, but which is extremely rough when fired. This causes the foot rims to scratch the surfaces wherever the ware is placed. Any suggestions?

The traditional solution has been to smooth the foot rim before firing, or to add felt pads to the bottoms of finished ware. However, there is another way—that is to grind the bottom smooth after firing. This can be done using an electric drill with a sanding disc; another solution is a glass grinder, the kind used to smooth the bottoms of handblown glass forms. The latter, a rather expensive machine, will mirror-polish foot rims even if they are covered with drips of glaze.

I have been destroying large bowls trying to find a good method for footing when the rim is larger than the wheel head or any available bat. Can you provide a suitable method?

Center a clay hump taller than the depth of the bowl to be footed. Remove excess water from the surface of the hump with a rib as the wheel turns at centering speed. Stop the wheel and invert the bowl on the hump as if it were a chuck. Neither bowl nor chuck should be so plastic or wet that the clay surfaces adhere to one another. The bowl may be centered and leveled with a tapping movement of the hand as the wheel slowly turns, and then footing may proceed in the usual manner. Once the chuck method is learned, footing time is significantly reduced, and the added support at the bottom of the form may reduce losses.

Drying

I get a small crescent-shaped crack in the center of the bottoms of about half my pots. I have made thick and thin bottoms, started using bats, dried fast, slow, upside down, and on slats of wood. Nothing has worked. Do you have any suggestions?

Caused by uneven compression between the walls and the bottom of the pot, the cracking may be corrected by throwing the hump down onto the wheel head before centering, although this practice may ultimately damage the wheel bearings. After the piece is firm and before trimming, the bottom can be compressed further by firmly striking the outside of the base with the fingers or the heel of the hand while the other hand supports the base from the inside. When throwing a plate, the fingers or a potter's rib can be pulled across the bottom both away from and toward the center several times to further increase the uneven compression caused by opening.

In making plates on the wheel (dinner, pie plates, etc.) I have a problem of the plates cracking while drying. After trimming they are set to dry in a temperature of 60° to 70°F. I have placed them on boards, on wires, on plaster,

on paper, face up and turned over. I use stoneware clay with varying amounts of grog; results: a ratio of one uncracked to five or six cracked. What must I do?

Try drying the plates very slowly, either in a damp box or under a plastic covering. We also would suggest that you place the plates on a thin layer of white sand or fine grog for drying, so that as the clay shrinks it will "roll" and be less likely to crack. In using this method, the initial drying would be face up.

I throw most of my pots from a large hump, Japanese style. As a result, some of my ware suffers from S-shaped cracks in the bottom. I read suggestions for curing this problem in Michael Cardew's text, *Pioneer Pottery*, and have been compressing the clay while throwing, but I still find that from 25% to 50% of my work is S-cracked. Sometimes the crack doesn't go completely through the bottom of the pot, and sometimes it does. Many times the crack doesn't appear until after the bisque or glaze firing. What else can I do to solve this problem?

There are excellent suggestions in the text you mention, but if you are still having problems it may be that you should try a clay body that is less plastic. Highly plastic bodies also shrink more and thus cause additional stress on the ware while drying. If your clay contains such plasticizers as bentonite or ball clay, you might try cutting down the amounts used. If a change in clay body does not solve your problem with cracks, there is one additional technique that you can try: Foot your ware when it is still relatively plastic, but before footing a pot, compress the bottom with a rib or your finger. This will relieve any stress that may have built up in that area. When footing is completed, compress again on the bottom as you did before. This should cut down your rate of cracking.

Decoration

I have been experimenting with sumi-e painting on my pots, but the commercial black stain I've been firing has a rather different quality from ink, and there are problems keeping it in suspension. The gray shades look especially ugly. Additionally, the bisqued pot quickly

sucks the brush dry, and won't allow the wash to run or bleed as on paper. Any advice?

Let's break your problem down into its two parts: the first problem is with the stain wash, and the second is with the pot to which it is applied.

The stain you're using is more coarse than sumi-e ink, and for this reason you might consider grinding the pigment with a mortar and pestle or ball mill before use. The more finely ground the stain, the more likely it is to give you the fully dispersed gray shades you are seeking. Mix 75 grams CMC gum in one gallon of water, and use this as a vehicle for your stain—the gum will help disperse and suspend the colorant. Or try sumi-e style painting on a background of wet slip in order to get any decoration to bleed more around the edges. Another approach to the problem is to switch from insoluble materials such as the stain you are now using to soluble colorants, as these naturally have the dispersed look of sumi-e painting. Soluble colorants, however, are relatively toxic and should be used only by those with a full knowledge of ceramic glaze chemistry. Manganese carbonate could be a good starting point for experimenting with soluble colorants, and this can be mixed with other solubles for further altering its overall hue. Or, any colorant, be it stain, oxide or carbonate, can be mixed with a lightweight oil instead of water, and the oil's viscosity can be regulated by cutting it with turpentine in the same manner as one cuts oil used in overglaze enameling. In this technique, the colorant is typically ground with the oil, and a very inklike quality can result. Oil-based-decoration will resist water-based glaze, however, and refiring to bisque temperatures may be necessary should you desire an overall glaze coat.

As to the problem with the pot pulling too much decorating liquid: in the case of water-based colorant media, the pot may simply be dipped in water prior to decoration, or the work can be bisqued to a higher temperature, which also may eliminate problems associated with body gases causing pinholing, cratering and other glaze defects.

Some combination of these suggestions should fit

your working methods, causing the least disruption to processes in which you have invested time and accumulated skill.

Can you explain how the treelike pattern on Mocha Ware is achieved?

Roger Little wrote about Mocha Ware in the January 1974 *Ceramics Monthly*: "First a cup of mocha tea is prepared. Two of the ingredients known to produce the mocha effect are tobacco and coffee. I usually use cigar stubs, but any form of tobacco will suffice. The tobacco is shredded and placed in a small pot, then just enough boiling water is added to cover the leaves. The resulting brew is steeped for an hour. The solution is then strained, the residue discarded, and a dark (ceramic) colorant is added to the 'tea.' Coloring oxides such as manganese, cobalt or any readily prepared underglaze color can be used. Copper oxide, however, is considered of little use since the pattern will diffuse in firing. The 'tea' is now ready to apply, although 24 hours maturing time will improve it.

"For application, the greenware is dipped in a contrasting color of slip. Plates and bowls can be covered by simply pouring the slip into them and draining just prior to decorating. Immediately, before the slip has a chance to set, the surplus is sponged from the base of the pot. The piece is next held in an inverted position and lightly touched near the base with a large, soft, banding brush charged with 'tea.' With deft manipulation of the pot and good brush control, the fluid will run down and spread rapidly, forming bare winter trees. A quick sideways stroke will join the trees into hedgerows."

How does one transfer silk-screened patterns onto curved, wet clay surfaces?

Instead of screening slip directly on clay, slip may be silk screened onto a thin plastic sheet, such as a dry-cleaning bag. The resultant pattern may be pressed slip-side down against wet ware, the clay manipulated in a manner appropriate to the pattern, and the plastic removed, leaving behind a serigraphic transfer. An inexpensive brand of syrup makes an excellent medium (in place of water) for mixing the slip.

Additional information is available in "Silk Screening with Slip," by Marvin Bartel, published in the March 1973 *Ceramics Monthly*.

I want to apply overglaze oxide brushwork in the majolica tradition, on a raw white glaze, but want a detailed pattern much like that achieved with underglaze. Do you have any suggestions?

After applying the base glaze, lay down areas of flat color in the usual manner. Then thinly spray the surface with a solution of gum tragacanth. Let the piece dry completely before decorating with detailed oxide or carbonate stains. For personalized results you will want to experiment with the strength of the gum solution, the amount of colorant used, and the dryness of the initial glaze surface.

A local art museum recently displayed a medieval Spanish pot decorated with a technique called *cuerda seca*. Do you know how this effect is achieved?

Traditionally, cuerda seca (dry cord) was a resist technique whereby manganese dioxide was mixed with oil and applied to ware in a decorative linear pattern. Various colors of glaze were then applied and resisted by the cuerda seca pattern, producing an effect similar to cloisonné enameling or a stained glass window.

Can you provide some information about the Japanese process called hakeme?

Hakeme is a type of brush decoration in which slip is applied to ware with a coarse brush. The resultant effect shows the marks of individual bristles through which body color can be seen. The technique often involves a strong contrast between body color and slip, and the latter may be applied loosely, in patterns or with the ware slowly turning on a banding wheel. While today it is associated with a number of well-known Japanese potters, the method dates to the Yi period in Korea. The success of the decoration involves both the skill of the potter and the composition of the brush. Coarse grasses may be tied together to form a successful brush, and Shoji Hamada is reputed to have used dog hair for hakeme application.

Decals

Recently my silk-screened ceramic decals have puddled or beaded during firings. I am using the materials and processes described in the April and May '75 *Ceramics Monthly*s ("Making Ceramic Decals" Parts I and II by Jonathan Kaplan). Can you suggest the causes for this?

The puddling in your decals is similar to crawling in glazes and can arise from having pigment or Clear Coat too thick. Try using less pigment first, then a thinner application of Clear Coat. A slower firing cycle may also help alleviate your problem.

Ceramics Monthly's **1975 April and May articles about making ceramic decals mentioned that full-color decals could also be fabricated. Do you have any information about this?**

With a color photo or transparency as subject matter, a commercial color separation can be purchased, and with proper registration of the silk screen (alignment of the image), color decals can be printed by use of the same techniques shown for black-and-white decal making in Jonathan Kaplan's articles.

A four-color separation can be commercially prepared by a color separator listed in the Yellow Pages of the phone book (or contact any medium to large printing company). When the separation is made, it will be four halftone negatives made from your one color image. Each is processed as if it were a black-and-white image as shown in the article. Then the resultant four silk screens are each printed with one color (red, blue, yellow and black).

Since color separation may be an expensive process, the potter might consider an alternative method. An imitation color image may sometimes be produced by printing twice with a single silk screen "halftone." The decal is first printed in black and then overprinted with a convincing color applied through the same screen, but with extremely slight variation in the registration or placement of the decal paper.

I have trouble with decals powdering off after firing. These particular decals are old; could that be the difficulty?

Ceramic materials are virtually ageless. If the decals haven't cracked or peeled, then they should be just as good today as when they were first made. If they powder off, it may be that you are not firing to a high enough temperature. It may also be that they were not properly made originally and do not contain enough flux to let them soften and become incorporated with the glaze underneath at the firing temperature.

Photographic Techniques

I recall reading about someone who was the first photoceramist. Will you refresh my memory and tell in detail about the earliest photoceramic processes?

In 1855 Lafon de Camarsac was the first to publish a method for producing permanent photographic images on vitrified porcelain. His miniature portraits fitted into lockets, brooches, pocket watches or small velvet-lined leather cases. Favorably compared with Sèvres paintings, the "burnt-in" images on porcelain and white enameled copper earned the French photographer a gold medal at the 1867 International Exhibition in Paris.

The original process was to transfer silver images with collodion film—collodion (on glass) being the commonly used photographic medium of the 1850s–1880s, consisting of a viscous solution of pyroxylin (soluble nitrocellulose) in a mixture of alcohol and ether or some other solvent. Because de Camarsac's porcelains were slightly curved, a collodion positive portrait had to be stripped from its support glass and the film carefully transferred. In the kiln, heat destroyed the collodion membrane and the oxidized silver left a yellow photographic image. For darker transfers, the film was treated with solutions of gold or platinum chlorides which react with silver, substituting their metal ions for the silver. The resultant monochrome portrait was thereafter fused to the porcelain with a thin layer of frit. Later, however, Lafon de Camarsac and others adopted a method utilizing the hygroscopic property (a light-sensitive tackiness) produced by photographically exposing a coating of iron perchloride and tartaric acid.

Patented in 1860 by Alphonse Poitevin, a chemist and civil engineer, the new process (which produced a good halftone image) was accomplished by exposing such a coating on unpolished glass through a negative. Then powdered carbon or other permanent pigment brushed on it would adhere only to those parts which had become sticky by exposure to the light, in concentrations according to the intensity of the light and consequent degree of stickiness. Covered with a layer of collodion and soaked in water, the image would detach from the glass and could be transferred to gelatinized paper (like that used for supporting decals today).

Lafon de Camarsac became a specialist in photoceramics and transferred images for other photographers throughout France and Europe. By the time he won the International Exhibition medal, he was credited with at least 15,000 ceramic photographs.

Is there another method of reproducing a photographic image on ceramic ware other than the photo silk-screen technique?

There are many variations on this technique, but one is significantly different. This process involves painting the ware under darkroom conditions with a liquid photo emulsion, exposing the pot as if it were a piece of sensitized paper, and developing it in the usual photo chemicals. Contact a photographic supply store for sources of specific products.

I saw a ceramic platter that was decorated with a photographic image. The decorating technique was described as "photo inlay." What are the basics of the process?

The photo inlay process is an interesting method that is related to the Japanese mishima technique. An image is deep-etched on a metal plate in the manner similar to letterpress engraving or the production of fine art etchings. Latex is cast over the plate and used as a rubber stamp to impress clay. The clay is covered with a different color slip and the form allowed to harden suitably until scraping the surface is possible.

As the clay surface is slowly planed away, the photographic image is revealed. After bisque firing, the clay is glazed with a clear recipe so the decoration will show through, or it may be salt glazed.

Wax Resist

Will wax resist or liquid wax applied to pots harm my kiln shelves during firing?

Wax products used to resist glaze on ware won't harm kiln shelves, but if liberally used on many pieces in the same firing, may cause a certain amount of reduction in an electric kiln if it is well sealed.

How is paraffin used for resist decoration, and is it easier to work with than wax emulsion?

Paraffin must be heated until it is very hot, then be used immediately while it still is in a liquid form. If the paraffin cools and stiffens as you work with it, it must be reheated. If a brush is used for applying the paraffin decoration, the brush should be cleaned immediately after use with kerosene so that all wax is removed. As you can see from this brief description, the use of hot paraffin is more complicated than the use of wax emulsion. In addition, there is an element of risk in heating paraffin and the chance that decorating brushes may be damaged or ruined.

FIRING

Stacking Ware

How far apart should ware be stacked for a glaze firing?

As ware is heated, it expands, and as glaze becomes molten, it bubbles out from the piece, so there is always a possibility that the glazes on two forms may touch each other. A distance of ¼ to ½ inch between works is about right.

I have been making some sculptural pots which rest on three points, but during firing, the points tend to warp

because the resistance of the weight of the piece on its points tends to prevent their movement while the rest of the pot shrinks. I've tried firing these pieces on sand, but even that doesn't help. What can I do to fire them without warping?

If your pots can be fired in another orientation—upside down, for example, that would be the simplest solution. But barring that, fire the pieces on a slab made of the same clay, and place the slab on a bed of sand to reduce shrinkage resistance from the kiln shelf. To be sure of success, the slab should accompany the pot through both bisque and glaze firings.

I have been making some 5-inch square tiles by the roll-and-cut method. These do not warp during the drying process but they invariably warp during the firing. I place them perfectly flat on the kiln shelves. Is this the best method for firing, or should I be doing something else?

Warping can be caused by so many forming factors that it would be difficult to pinpoint the trouble without observing your studio processes. It's possible that the lack of circulation around the tiles might be the problem. Try standing the tiles on end during drying, and purchase a firing rack designed especially for this job, so that each tile receives even heat and good circulation during firing.

Is it safe to fire pieces for bisque and glaze in the kiln at the same time?

It is safe to fire bisque and glaze pieces together if you are certain of the construction of the pieces that are being bisque fired. It is best to separate bisque and glaze pieces in the kiln to prevent any glaze volatilization from attacking the bisque and thus forming vitreous areas. Such areas would be most difficult to glaze. If your kiln is a larger one, it may have hot and cool sections. If so, the bisque can be stacked in the cooler section and the glazed ware in the hotter area.

I occasionally find it useful to stilt ware which is being fired with overglazes. But it is always a problem getting the work properly situated on the stilt when loading the

kiln. Do you have any ideas for keeping ware in place?

Stilts may be glued in place for easy loading of ware; the adhesive burns out during firing.

Firing Ware

We are firing to Cone 08 for bisqueware, which is then dip glazed. But this seems unsatisfactory for brush glazing, because the pot quickly sucks up all the moisture before a reasonable brushstroke can be achieved. I also sense that our glaze pitting is related to bisque firing, because of sulfur release. How does one determine appropriate bisque temperature for a specific body and for potential methods of glazing and decoration?

Proper temperature for this first firing can solve a variety of glaze defects, though contemporary potters have tended to accept a rather modern tradition of bisque firing between Cones 08 and 04.

Historically, though, bisque firing has run the gamut from extremely low temperatures to the high vitrification range of porcelain. If potters experimented more with bisque temperatures, they would undoubtedly find more consistent and satisfactory results in the final glaze firing. Some other ideas to consider: As bisque temperatures rise, porosity decreases, as does the resultant wet glaze suction of the body. Equally important is the fact that higher bisque temperatures release greater quantities of gas which would otherwise have to escape during glaze firing—thereby creating pinholes and sometimes cratering. Some materials released from the body (such as sulfur) may have drastic effects on the glaze surface and quality, at least in sufficient quantities. Yet the bisque firing range from Cone 08 to 04 may be insufficient to cure most sulfur problems, particularly in a purely oxidation firing when sulfuric oxide is the cause. Thus, the bisque is typically determined as the lowest temperature firing (for purposes of energy efficiency) at which desirable effects are achieved.

When glaze is applied by spray gun, very low bisque firing is an advantage because the surface dries quickly—immediately ready for the next coat, lacking unwanted drips. When a glaze is applied by dipping, bisque firing may be raised to a higher temperature, and for brushing, even higher. Suction of the body may be reduced additionally by dipping or spraying it with water before glaze application. Glazes to be dipped may additionally be thinned excessively to compensate for extremely porous bisqueware.

Glazes containing sufficient quantities of soluble materials (ash glazes or those with soluble colorants such as the metallic chlorides and nitrates) may be greatly affected by the amount of porosity resulting from a previous bisque firing. The greater the porosity (lower the bisque) the more matt the ash glaze and the more soluble colorants bleed through the ware.

Determining an appropriate bisque temperature can be quickly achieved after a series of bisque firings to various cones in a small test kiln. Because of the many variables, potters must determine empirically their own best bisque temperature—no single prescription is sufficient.

I would like to know the general process of stoking a wood-fired kiln.

Very dry and well-seasoned wood cut from 2–8 inches in diameter by 2–2½ feet long (or in lengths to fit the firebox) are generally used, with smaller, thinner kindling burned toward the end of the firing. At first, several pieces of wood are burned to coals in the firebox. This may take up to 30 minutes, at which time more wood is added to the coals remaining on the grate. As the temperature rises the stoking rate increases; progressively thinner wood is added.

The kiln atmosphere changes throughout the stoking sequence: with the burst of flame and smoke from the new wood, there is a reducing condition changing to neutral after the initial burning, and as the wood burns to coals, the atmosphere becomes oxidizing. Reduction can be maintained through this cycle by partially closing off the damper at the chimney, although too much damping can retard the temperature rise or even cause the kiln to lose heat. Cleaning the ash pit during firing can alter the amount of air being drawn into the kiln and can also cause heat loss. A properly stoked kiln should produce little ash, making cleaning unnecessary.

Pine burns the hottest because of its resin content and open-cell structure; fine splitting exposes more surface to the heat, promoting combustion. Pine produces more smoke yet promotes an oxidizing atmosphere overall. Hardwoods also burn well and produce less smoke, while tending to cause a reducing atmosphere. Wood may be inexpensively obtained from city maintenance departments as fallen trees and limbs, from manufacturing companies, lumberyards as scrap, and sawmills in the form of slab wood. Kilns vary and this fact combined with the type of ware, the peak temperatures desired, and kiln atmosphere will make some experimentation necessary to determine an efficient firing schedule.

I have been trying to fire a wood-burning kiln and have been having difficulty with stoking. The firing is very erratic even though I am using a good grade of dry firewood. Peak temperature is hard to reach even though I'm certain the kiln is built right. Does the size of wood have much to do with good stoking?

If you are not grading your wood by size, this could be your problem, although specific kiln firings hold many variables. Stoking with wood usually begins with the largest pieces since they burn more slowly. These are followed later in the firing with smaller pieces until during the last part of the firing some potters use the smallest twigs, with larger pieces thrown on the fire for reduction.

We live in an area that has a lot of coal, and I would like to use this fuel to fire our kiln. Any suggestions for firing with coal such as type, glazes, grate composition, etc.?

The best place to learn about coal firing is from someone still firing a traditional coal-fueled kiln. In your region, there may yet be some brickyards firing with coal, and you can learn a lot if you can arrange to be around when brick is "burned." Bituminous coal is usually burned in ceramic kilns, and the firebox grates are modified to withstand the hotter (than wood) burning temperatures by closer spacing of iron bars, or grates constructed of fireclay. Because of the sulfur content in most coal (which causes glaze scumming) and because coal ash leaves coarse deposits on ware, pots fired with this fuel are stacked in saggars (clay boxes) to protect them from the kiln atmosphere. *The Kiln Book,* by Fred Olsen, contains a variety of references to coal firing, including kiln plans for the Delhi Blue Pottery's large coal-fired kiln in New Delhi, India. Smaller kilns could be adapted from this design.

Nearly everything I read about firing recommends a slow period of heating up the kiln for firing ceramics. My old kiln, which is a small one, has just one switch, and therefore I can't leave it on "low" for several hours before switching it to "high." Do you have any suggestions on how I can slow down the firing with such a kiln?

There are several recommendations we can make. Leave the peephole plug out and leave the door slightly ajar for the first hour or two of firing in order to lengthen the firing time. You also can turn the switch on, leave it on for about ten minutes, then turn it off and leave it off for about ten to twenty minutes, then repeat this for the first hour or two of firing before finally leaving the switch on, the peephole plug in and the door closed. This is a rather time-consuming process, but it might give you better firing results.

One of the many confusing things about ceramics is the material I read concerning firing temperature and firing time. It seems to me that if the kiln is fired to the proper temperature as indicated by the melting of the cone, the amount of firing time would be unimportant. Any comments?

Time is of almost equal importance to heat in firing ceramic pieces. During the watersmoking period, from the start of firing to dull red heat, the chemically combined water and carbonaceous matter in the clay must be expelled slowly to avoid damage to the ware. For thin-walled pieces, the firing time should be no less than 90 minutes; for sculpture and pottery with thick walls, a considerably longer time should be taken. If the temperature rises too fast, breakage or bloating may result.

During the period of firing when the ware approaches the maturing temperature, both time and temperature are necessary for uniform shrinkage throughout the structure of the piece. Many potters hold the kiln temperature at the maturing temperature for a short period at the end of the firing. This gives greater vitrification and more even penetration of heat and results in a much better fired body.

Electric Reduction

In *Ceramics Monthly*'s April 1983 issue, an article about Beatrice Wood mentions use of a "smoking stick" for reduction firing in an electric kiln. Can you explain more fully? I would be most interested in a generic version rather than her technique specifically. Does this smoke firing harm the electric kiln? Does it affect future firing?

Beatrice Wood uses a variation of the traditional Arabian luster technique, wherein a combustible material is introduced into the firing chamber at some point after reaching peak temperature (with the electricity shut off), and continuing until the last color of radiant energy inside the firing chamber disappears. Either charcoal or wood is commonly used in sufficient quantities to produce sooty black smoke inside (and emanating from) the kiln. The combustible material is simply pushed through one of the lower peepholes into a temporary firebox or bisqued bowl placed on the kiln floor to protect it from wood ash deposits. Reduction lusters which are created by this process have a unique sheen caused by starving oxygen from the glaze's metallic oxides. While no special wood is required, sticks of dry resinous pine work especially well. An oxidation firing following each smoke firing is recommended to reestablish the protective oxide layer on the kiln's electric elements. Nevertheless, there is evidence that element life may be shortened somewhat by luster glaze firings (although to the best of our knowledge, no definitive studies exist on element life and severe carbonization). While all electric kilns ought to have adequate ventilation, reduced luster requires extensive ventilation, since carbon dioxide and carbon monoxide may result.

A truly generic, traditional (and poisonous) Arabian luster glaze is fired in a fuel-burning kiln and consists of alum, mercuric sulfide, red iron oxide and silver sulfide mixed with vinegar. To illustrate the breadth of the technique, compare this composition with Beatrice Wood's recipes published in the article you mention. In any case, when the smoked surfaces are removed from the kiln, they typically require abrasive polishing to reveal the resulting sheen.

Finally, it should be noted that reduced luster firings can be tricky, and do not always succeed. For this reason, commercial luster glazes which can be fired in oxidation provide a more reliable although considerably more expensive alternative.

Someone said mothballs in the kiln during glaze firing will produce iridescence. True or false?

A modified true. Introducing mothballs into a kiln during the cooling period produces a smoky, or reduction, atmosphere that will give an iridescent effect better known as luster to certain glazes. However, the use of mothballs to induce reduction in electric kilns is not recommended, as fumes may be harmful to the elements, and the napthalene causes a strong blow-back flame. It is better to introduce smoking sticks or a few small pieces of charcoal instead.

Once Firing

I know that many professional potters omit bisque firing and fire their ware only once. There seems to be very little written about this. I have been experimenting on my own but with very poor results. Often the small test tiles turn out well, but when I try the same glaze on a larger piece it invariably crawls. In my case firing is done in a gas kiln and I am most interested in glazes maturing at Cones 5–7.

Single firing is quite practical for the ceramist. Your problem seems to be one of using comparatively nonplastic glazes on highly plastic clay bodies. In such cases the clay may shrink over 10% in the drying and firing, and the applied glaze shrink only a fraction of this. This causes cracks to appear in the glaze which may be too wide to heal over during the firing and in this manner cause crawling. The solution is to use more plastic glazes containing higher proportions of clay than are usually included in glazes to be used on bisque ware. You might try the following glazes for Cones 5–7:

Single-Fire Glaze I (Cone 5–7)

Borax (sieved to 100 mesh)	25 %
Lithium Carbonate	25
Ball Clay	50
	100 %

Single-Fire Glaze II (Cone 5–7)

Gerstley Borate	50 %
Ball Clay	50
	100 %

If either is too runny in the firing, increase the ball clay somewhat. If too matt or stony, decrease the clay content.

Is pottery that is given two firings—a bisque and a glaze—stronger than pottery that is single fired?

Single-fired pottery should be just as strong and durable as pottery that has been given two firings. Its strength depends on how much heat the clay has been exposed to, not how many times it has been fired. The use of pottery depends also on the success of the glaze cover. A glaze without defects gives additional strength and usefulness to a fired object.

Vapor Glazing

After salt glazing pots for many years, I would like to begin producing salt-glazed ware without the traditional orange-peel surface. How can the potter achieve a smooth, shiny surface with salt?

Following salting the kiln 2 or 3 times in the normal manner, add about 5–10% borax to the salt for subsequent saltings. The final "salting" should consist completely of borax.

We have been experimenting with the use of bicarbonate of soda as a substitute when salt glazing. In an effort to save fuel, we wish to "salt" at an efficient temperature. Can you make some recommendations?

Finding the most efficient temperature is highly dependent on the vitrification point of your clay body. Bodies nearing maturity will more freely bond their alumina and silica to the soda in the atmosphere, thus forming a glaze coating.

An article by Anne Shattuck in the British magazine *Pottery Quarterly* relates, "When the sodium bicarbonate was introduced before 1240°C, the clay was not mature enough to take the soda. 1260°C was found to be the best time to start, stretching the soda period over two to three hours until (1300°C was reached).... We had the best results when the kiln was completely closed off from escaping gases during the introduction of soda. Since soda, when volatilizing, doesn't move as readily through the kiln as salt, it is important to keep the secondary air ports closed. This increases pressure and insures a soda-saturated atmosphere."

Raku

A friend and I have a long-standing dispute about who originated raku in the United States, and when. He contends that Paul Soldner was the originator of the American version of this Oriental process and philosophy, but I feel that it had earlier American advocates. Who is right?

Warren Gilbertson is credited with the introduction of raku to this country in 1941. Having returned from a trip to Japan, he exhibited 250 pots at the Art Institute of Chicago, and a number of them were raku.

Can you provide me with information on salt-fired raku? When and how is the salt used?

Salt-fired raku currently takes a number of forms. Some potters are introducing salt into the raku kiln with unglazed ware, and the material selectively stains the body. The usual result in this case is not a glassy surface, but rather an effect like sprayed oxide wash. In a variation, salt may be thrown on glazed ware during raku firing to alter the qualities of the surface through a sodium addition. Another method employs a mixture of salt and borax, or borax alone, which is thrown into the raku kiln directly on unglazed ware, glazing that portion where the compound falls. Borax is added as an active flux and glass former, which reduces the melting point of salt so that both compounds may actively attack clay or glaze surfaces in proportion to kiln temperature.

I've read that one can be electrocuted by a rush of charged, super-heated air when rakuing in an electric kiln. Is this true? Can you explain how raku can be done safely in an electric kiln?

One cannot be electrocuted by hot air from an electric kiln, regardless of its temperature, as air resists the passage of electrical current. But one can certainly be burned by sufficient heat from any kiln, be it electric, gas, wood, etc. Raku ware can be produced safely in an electric kiln by shutting off the electrical power to the elements, provided the kiln is well grounded and you are not a better ground than the kiln's. An even safer method was outlined in the October 1974 issue of *Ceramics Monthly* (p. 43) and the January 1979 issue (p. 52), wherein a muffle is constructed to fit about 1½ inches from the kiln elements, making it impossible for tongs to contact elements, and also to protect the firing chamber from contact with glaze.

Refiring

I would appreciate any help on how to fire overglaze colors on stoneware without body cracking. My normal firing is to turn the kiln for 30 minutes on low, 30 minutes on medium, and 30 minutes on high, all with the lid raised 2 inches, then closing the lid with a usual total firing time of about 2 hours. I have tried stilting the ware for better circulation under the foot, inverting ware so that the heavier foot is in the upper part of the kiln, and even changing the firing sequence from 30 minutes to 1 hour on low, medium and high. When a piece cracks on the first firing, I usually consider it faulty, but when it cracks on the second or third firing, I feel I am not doing something right. What is the correct procedure?

Your firing cycle seems too fast, and this is the probable cause of the problem you mention, as well-made ware should be firable a variety of times without cracking. "Well made" in this case means pieces not under unusual stress from glaze/body fit differentials or from "clay memory" or excessively uneven drying prior to the bisque firing. Given these considerations, the next most important caution is that the work be well dried after overglaze colors have been applied, as the first thousand degrees are especially critical for the removal of mechanically and chemically held water. A good test to see if water is causing your problem is to turn the kiln on low for an hour with the lid propped open 1 inch; let the ware sit in this environment overnight or for a few hours before starting the regular firing cycle. One hour each on low, medium and high should be sufficient, but if the ware is thick or uneven, more time is required on low in order to prevent cracking. To be safe, try three hours on low, then proceed one hour on medium and then turn the kiln to high until shutoff. If ware still cracks, keep adding half-hour increments to the first phase of the cycle to see if you can prevent cracking with still slower firing. (Fast firing is the usual cause of cracking in overglaze firing: the ware simply doesn't have time to evenly absorb heat, and thus unresolved stresses are produced.)

Two mugs I recently glazed had some bare spots on the inside which I didn't notice until after they had been used for food. How can I clean these areas? I want to be sure all the grease is removed so I can reglaze the mugs.

The best way to thoroughly clean any piece of ware preparatory to glazing or reglazing is to fire it to a dull red heat. All impurities will burn out in just a short time.

Cooling

We have a Fiberfrax kiln in which we fire a variety of ware—sometimes large planters, at other times hundreds of small pieces. Some of our matt glazes appear to be strongly affected by the kind of load we fire them in. Can you explain this or offer a solution?

Kilns built of refractory fiber tend to cool according to the mass of ware contained inside. Thus your loads of small pieces tend to have more mass than a load of a few large pieces. When mattness in glaze is caused by a high alumina content, the recipe tends to be sensitive to the rate of cooling. Thus your three options are to switch to matt glazes which are not dependent on high alumina, to attempt to more closely control the rate of cooling by equalizing the fired mass, or to fire down.

What is the quickest cooling schedule that can be used for a forced-air gas kiln with a capacity of about 25 cubic feet? Mine seems to cool from about 2000°F to 1000°F in four hours and then takes 24 hours to cool to 400°F (which is as long as I can wait). Can I open the damper at 1000°F and then take out the two doors at 500°F?

The safest practice for any kiln, either gas or electric, and for the ware, is to allow it to cool for a period as long as the firing time. It should be safe to open the damper when the kiln has cooled down to 1000°F. It would be best to merely "crack" the doors at 400° or 500°F, then wait several hours before removing them completely.

I have a portable gas updraft kiln with single-wall construction and six small burners at the bottom. Once maturing temperature (Cone 9 for glaze and Cone 04 for bisque) is reached and the kiln turned off, heat loss is so rapid that pots crack and sometimes break. I wonder about using a hiker's "moonblanket" which has a metal foil side and wrapping it around the kiln to reflect heat and slow cooling. Any suggestions on how the problem can be solved?

The problem exists in gas-fired as well as some electric kilns. One sure way to extend the cooling period is to continue "firing down" after the maturing temperature of the glaze has been reached by leaving burners or electric elements on a lower setting than that used to reach peak temperature. In the absence of a pyrometer, the temperature drop can be monitored by observing the color of the kiln interior at intervals. One possible guideline for slow cooling is to supply heat to the kiln for about one half of the time it took to go from bisque to final temperature.

Refractory insulation may be added to some kilns and is available from ceramics suppliers in paper, blanket and board forms. However, the use of the "moonblanket" does not seem desirable. The foil side would reflect some heat but as the blanket was not designed to withstand more than low temperatures, there may be a hazard created by wrapping it around the kiln.

Heat Measuring Devices

In regard to the pyrometer, should the needle rest at zero before the kiln is turned on or should it register the same as room temperature? I never have the feeling of absolute security that the pyrometer is registering the same as cones might, and consequently am inclined to blame glaze failures on inaccurate firing.

The pyrometer needle should register the same as room temperature, which usually is about 70°F. If your pyrometer registers at zero, this might very well account for your glaze failures. Pyrometers are sensitive instruments and they should be checked periodically for accuracy. If you find that the pyrometer reading is inaccurate, the needle can be reset by a slight turn of the screw on the pyrometer face.

Is it necessary to use cones or is a pyrometer sufficient? Some friends of mine fire by the clock and seem to do quite well.

Cones are very inexpensive and can spell the difference between a good firing and a failure. When you consider the tremendous amount of work that goes into a full kiln load of ware, the low cost of a cone seems insignificant.

Firing is a time-temperature proposition. Clay and glaze must be slowly raised to a given temperature over a period of time in order to mature. The exact time and temperature will vary with the amount of pieces in the kiln, the rate of temperature rise, and many other factors. A cone is subjected to the same conditions as the ware in the kiln, so it tells the exact story regarding maturity.

A pyrometer tells only temperature; a clock tells

only time. Put the two of them together and you have a cone. Why not take the easy way out and use a cone?

I can't figure out why the kiln sitter in my electric kiln does not shut off whenever a shelf is horizontally aligned with it, even though there appears to be sufficient space between the shelf and the sitter before firing. Do you have any information about this?

A representative of the Edward Orton, Jr., Ceramic Foundation (Columbus, Ohio) comments that this is not an uncommon problem with kiln sitters, and recommends the shelf be placed no closer than one inch above or below the kiln sitter bar. The cause of your problem is thermal expansion of the shelf, which can be sizable—sufficient to close the gap in question—thus preventing the bar above the cone from tripping the shut-off switch.

Cones

What is the proper position for a cone when it is "down"— is it lying down flat, bent halfway over or just starting to bend?

A cone is considered "down" when it has bent over in a smoothly curved arch and its tip is parallel to the top of the plaque in which the cone is embedded.

I understand that cones measure heat work (a temperature-time relationship) rather than simply temperature alone. Yet when one compares the way small and large cones of the same numerical designation behave in the kiln, there is quite a difference. Can you explain this and show the relationship of small and large cones fired at the same temperature and rate?

The answer to your question is a complex one. To begin with, small and large cones of the same number are made from the same material composition, but there the similarity ends. "Though the viscosity of both large and small cones [standing inclined at 8° from vertical] would decrease at nearly the same rate when heated side by side, the greater weight of the large cone will cause it to deform first," stated a representative of the Orton Foundation staff. What's more, there are other variables: a small cone used horizontally in a kiln sitter deforms earlier than the same cone standing 8° from vertical primarily because of the added weight of the sitter bar. The deformation is further influenced by factors including the position of the cone beneath the kiln sitter tripping bar, and the adjustment of the kiln sitter. (Orton found three different weights of kiln sitter bars on three kilns tested; the bars weighed 3.4, 3.8 and 3.6 grams respectively, at the point of contact. Most kiln sitters are adjustable by moving the tripping mechanism on the outside end of the kiln sitter bar.)..."Contributing as much to the nonprescriptive nature of this cone comparison are the temperature variations found in every kiln," said an Orton source.

With all these variables, it should not be surprising that Orton has no charts which compare small and large cones fired at the same rate. The only useful comparison for the potter is to fire large and small cones side by side in the same manner in which you use them. Orton states, "this actual performance test is probably more helpful than temperature data."

Generally speaking, though, small cones will deform at approximately 15°C higher than the corresponding large cones when fired in the recommended near-vertical position. When the small cone is fired horizontally in a kiln sitter, it generally shuts off electrical current from one to one and a half cones lower than the corresponding near-vertical large cone.

After the last heavy rain, water seeped into my basement wetting a whole box of nearly 50 pyrometric cones. I've dried them out, but will they now fire accurately?

Cones which have been wet may lose their original dry pressed strength and crack during firing, rather than bending. Thus they may indicate a temperature/time relationship somewhat less than the cone number. To determine if the cones are damaged, test fire some random samples from the previously damp cones against examples not exposed to dampness.

Charts for pyrometric cones list peak firing temperatures based on the rate of heat increase per hour. Since my

firing involves different rates of firing at various times during the cycle, may I average these to find the actual temperature to which I fire?

Only the rate of increase at the end of the firing cycle affects the cone. Fast or slow firing at the beginning or middle of the cycle has no bearing on the temperature at which the cone will bend.

Can cones which didn't bend over in a firing be used again?

Heat from the first firing causes enough change in the cones to make them unreliable for reuse.

Did traditional American folk potters ever make their own pyrometric cones?

Pyrometric cones have been considered a relatively recent addition to the potter's heat and time indicators, but *Pottery Collectors' Newsletter* reports that the Meaders' pottery in White County, Georgia, made cones from the glazes used in each particular firing. Melting of the cone indicated that the glazes had melted too. These cones were used in the traditional "groundhog kiln," typical of many American folk potteries.

I note that a small cone installed in an electric kiln sitter can be fired with larger and smaller cross sections underneath the sitter trip bar. Would you tell me how much variation this placement can make?

While it depends on the number of the cone used, the average difference is approximately three-fourths of a cone from the smallest cross section to the largest, provided that the cone is properly installed.

FIRED WARE

Finishing Touches

I am making stoneware bottles with cork stoppers and wish the corks could be made to fit better. Is there a good way other than turning them on a lathe?

The grinder found in most studios for smoothing

foot rims, or removing a glaze drip makes a great cork shaper for custom fitting the stopper to a bottle neck.

I've noticed some potters' jar lids fit almost as if they've been ground smooth—a very pleasant sensation. How is this quality achieved?

In some cases, they actually have been ground. Sanding before firing is sometimes practiced. But the best solution is an application of any oil (3-in-1 is a good choice) and a very fine grit silicon carbide placed on the rim. Twist the lid back and forth in place, thereafter wiping the oil/grit residue from the rim. This technique works quickly and effectively.

Photographing Work

I want to take my own 35mm slides for entering juried shows and crafts fairs. Additionally, I would like to produce my own publicity photographs—8×10 black-and-white glossies and color transparencies. Can you recommend a specific camera or cameras to meet these needs, or should I hire a professional?

Ceramics Monthly tested a variety of single lens reflex 35mm cameras ranging in price from a few thousand dollars (Leica) to a few hundred dollars (Canon). Kodachrome 25 transparency film was chosen for its fine grain structure; the same roll was wound from camera to camera. Exposures were made of a test grid as well as actual ceramic works set up for taking museum-quality slides. Optimum exposure circumstances were used in order to get the best photos capable of being made by each camera: f/16 for ½ second using a tripod and cable release along with studio lighting.

Surprisingly, no visible qualitative difference could be found between transparencies shot with the various cameras, even though there were several thousand dollars' difference in price among them. Even after making 8×10 blowups of these transparencies, no visible qualitative difference could be found. There were some slight differences in rendition of color from lens to lens, some extremely slight differences in shutter speed, but these were all relatively insignificant.

Thus, we advise potters to buy an inexpensive 35mm single lens reflex camera with a 50mm to 60mm macro lens instead of the standard lens. This equipment should be sufficient for producing 35mm slides for shows and fairs. For larger transparencies (for gallery presentations, book and magazine publication), and for shooting good quality black-and-white glossy prints, a medium-format (2¼-inch square) or large-format (4×5-inch) camera is recommended. Here again, the condition of the equipment is more important than its brand or price, and equipment with macro capability is more versatile (allowing for close-ups as well as standard views).

The photographic artist's knowledge, talent and skill are more important than the equipment used. And there is as broad a range of creativity in photography as there is in ceramics. Good professional photographers will doubtless be able to produce better images than the ceramist; it's their specialty, so hire a qualified professional product photographer for best results. Judge a photographer's talent by her/his portfolio. If you don't see images therein which satisfy the way you want your work presented, seek another photographer who meets your criteria.

Before a recent exhibition of my work, the gallery owners asked me to provide all the black-and-white publicity photos. Is this a common practice? Should I hire a professional photographer? What kind of photos should I send?

The best galleries provide the ceramist with services in addition to selling work, and among these is the publicizing of an exhibition in newspapers and magazines. Such galleries take and distribute publicity photos primarily of individual works on plain backgrounds to help insure favorable media coverage. The gallery occasionally will request additional photos from the artist when these deal with subjects to which a gallery photographer does not have reasonable access—photos of the artist working in a distant studio, photos of earlier times, etc.

There are exceptions, however, and many professional-quality galleries vary in photographic policy.

Some artists, on the other hand, prefer to manage all their own publicity in order to control the way their work is presented in public. When this is the case, ceramists generally engage a professional photographer in whom they have confidence. Regardless of the source of photography, be it the gallery or the artist, most publishers of exhibition reviews and publicity would recommend using a professional photographer whenever practical. The standard of publicity photos is usually an 8×10-inch, glossy, black-and-white. In instances where high-quality color reproduction is a possibility, color transparencies (which look like big slides) are used most often in the 4×5-inch size.

Packing and Shipping

We produce and ship a line of bottles with fragile, slim necks. Our problem is excessive breakage of the necks, even though they are well packed. Could you advise some economically feasible method of preventing this?

Fragile, protruding forms are often a problem for the potter when it comes to shipping. An inexpensive and successful technique has been used by studio potters who invert disposable plastic cups over fragile parts of the ware, secured with masking tape. These protective cups (like those that airlines use to serve drinks) are economical, surprisingly strong when in place and come in a variety of sizes. They are available at most grocery and discount stores.

I have been searching for good containers for shipping pots to exhibitions. Since the work is generally returned after showing, the container must be relatively permanent and reusable. Any suggestions?

One of the best reusable containers is the commercially manufactured fiber drum with a metal lid and rims at the top and bottom. Fiber drums are exceptionally strong and come in a variety of sizes from small "hatboxes" to large drums in excess of 50 gallons. Many large manufacturers as well as ceramic suppliers receive goods in this type of container and occasionally may release these without charge. An-

170

other good source might be the "Barrels and Drums" section listed in the telephone book Yellow Pages.

Laying Tile

I just completed a tile mural commission, and now am about to install it myself. Everything is worked out, except for an efficient way to guarantee that the tiles are spaced properly, as the architect demands that grout space be equal throughout. Is there any professional method for installing tiles with equal space between them on a vertical wall surface?

Professional installers often stick up tiles with a piece of rope between them in order to reserve equal grout space. This rope can be simply pulled free after the tiles have set, then grout added where the rope used to be. In extremely critical areas, small scrap wood shims can be added on top of the rope to slightly increase space. Rope between the tiles will even allow the artist an opportunity to quickly and accurately lay the mural out on the studio floor after firing for a last minute check of dimensions prior to shipping or installation.

I would like to make tiles for my bathroom walls and floor. Could you provide some information on body and glaze requirements, as well as formulas for mortar and grout?

Tile bodies should be sufficiently hard to withstand typical floor abrasion. But even earthenware, when fired near its peak temperature, will suffice. The glaze on floor tile should contain enough alumina and silica to be excessively hard; avoid extremely glassy surfaces for functional safety, except with very gritty tile bodies. Wall tile, while not requiring the same hardness as that used on the floor, is often glazed for easy cleaning.

According to the Tile Council of America, floor tile is generally laid in a thick layer of mortar consisting of 1 part portland cement to 6 parts sand; for walls use portland cement, sand and hydrated lime in proportions from 1:5½:1 to 1:7:1. The mortar bed for either floors or walls should be from ¾ to 1 inch overall, and can be reinforced with metal lath, mesh, or can be backed with a vapor-proof membrane. This mortar is not affected by water and can be used to plumb and level surfaces. Suitable backings include brick or cement masonry, concrete, wood frame, rough wood floors, plywood floors, foam insulation board, gypsum board, portland cement and gypsum plaster.

A mixture of 1 part portland cement to 1 part fine-graded sand is used for grouting ceramic mosaic tile. A mixture of 1 part portland cement to 2 parts fine-graded sand (to which ⅕ part lime may be added) is used for quarry tile. Damp curing is necessary.

There are many other types of mortars, adhesives and grout available. Consult your local building supply for additional information and your local code for special requirements.

SAFETY

Raw Materials

I am apprenticing with a master potter who has asked me to research toxic substances in the studio. I have seen the various articles and comments in *Ceramics Monthly* and other publications, and am aware of the individual materials which are supposed to be toxic, but I am concerned about whether combinations of these materials (formed in liquid glaze or as glaze dust) might pose new hazards about which we are unaware. Is there some government agency charged with helping us make this kind of determination?

According to a recent edition of the federal government's "Toxic Substances List," the evaluation of hazards in the workplace and the technology for their control are the principal responsibility of the National Institute for Occupational Safety and Health (NIOSH). However, some people in business, including studio potters, have felt there to be risks in contacting NIOSH, out of fear of excessive regulation, or the inability to meet NIOSH standards. Regardless of this extenuating circumstance, NIOSH makes a convincing case in warning of the complexity in understanding ceramic and other toxicological effects: "A critical evaluation of a chemical hazard involves much more than a determination of the toxic potency, no matter how complex the determination may be. A hazard evaluation must include such a determination, of course, but toxic potency and hazardousness cannot be considered as being synonymous. Identifying and defining a chemical hazard must also include the evaluation of the amount and duration of exposure, the physical characteristics of the substance, the physical condition under which exposure occurs and determination of the presence of other chemical substances. All of these may significantly alter the toxic potency of a substance which, in turn, may alter the health and behavior of the human who may be exposed.

"Ventilation, appropriate hygienic practice, good housekeeping, protective clothing and pertinent training for safe handling may mediate any hazard that might exist. Hazard evaluation requires, therefore, engineers, chemists, toxicologists and physicians, who have been trained in the field of toxicology...and occupational health to recognize, measure and control these hazards."

I've read about the dangers of lead glazes in pots, but would like to know the danger of working with lead to potters who formulate their own glazes. What precautions should be taken?

Lead is a cumulative poison. If taken in sufficient doses or in small doses over a period of time, lead quantities may add up to a toxic level in the body. To be dangerous to the human anatomy, lead must be soluble like white lead, red lead, litharge, lead chromate, etc. Properly formulated lead silicates contain a balance of silica, alumina and lead flux so that all free lead is used up to form the glaze matrix. These silicates are then insoluble and thus rendered safe. Potters should avoid all contact with soluble lead. Lead enters the body by being absorbed through the skin, inhaled or ingested. Those working near lead compounds should not mix glazes with bare hands, and should neither transport nor weigh glazes where skin would be in contact with lead. Lead dust should be kept to a minimum and an approved dust mask should be worn when working with lead. During kiln firings, make every attempt to keep kiln fumes away from people when lead is present in firing glazes. Always wash your hands thoroughly after working with lead compounds.

If there is any question about whether a lead compound is soluble or not, consider it soluble. If you use prepared frits or glazes and don't know if they contain lead, consult the manufacturer. Even if a frit or commercial glaze contains only "safe" compounds, ball milling or the addition of certain colorants may render the mixture unsafe. If you feel you might have lead poisoning, consult your doctor. It can be tested for painlessly.

Will you please list chemical elements other than lead which may be potentially harmful to potters, and symptoms which might signal overexposure? What precautions should be taken in the studio?

Experts seem to disagree about which materials in what form and what quantities may be harmful to potters, but elements that generally are mentioned include antimony, barium, cadmium, chromium, cobalt, selenium, uranium and vanadium. There is agreement that asbestos products are especially hazardous in the studio. There may be other hazardous individual materials; combinations of materials remain virtually unstudied.

In a publication released by Hazards in the Arts, 15 symptoms of overexposure are listed: headache, dizziness, blurred vision, bad taste in the mouth, general fatigue, nausea, vomiting, nervousness, loss of appetite, chronic cough, dermatitis, irritability, skin discoloration, depression and shortness of breath. Always consult your doctor about such health questions.

Among precautions for the studio, the following should be of note to potters: Don't smoke. If you do, avoid smoking and working at the same time. Work in a well-ventilated studio; keep clothes and the work area clean, and wet mop to avoid excess dust. Wear a protective breathing device when dust is unavoidable. Keep food and food containers separate from the work area; wash hands before leaving the studio. Keep children out of the work area when using hazardous materials.

I am planning to build a house/studio with forced-air heating throughout, but recently I have heard that dust from a ceramics studio will clog the heating system. What can I do?

Clay and glaze dust will not clog a typical heating system, although it may be necessary to change the furnace filter more frequently. But health experts agree that breathing ceramic dust should be kept to a minimum.

A simple solution to the tracking of dust on shoes or feet is to place a doormat at every studio exit, and to keep the work area relatively clean when work is finished. Dust in the air is a more complex problem. One solution is that the studio should not have a cold air return duct, but should be equipped with an exhaust fan which pulls slightly more air than that blown into the room by the hot air vent. The exhaust fan might be connected to the same electrical circuit as the furnace fan. Exhausting air from the studio creates negative pressure in the work area, constantly drawing clean air into the room.

Kiln Emissions

I have a very good quality respirator (NIOSH approved) for dust removal, and would like to know if this is good protection when salt glazing. I have heard both sides on salt kiln fumes from horror stories to comments that the kiln gases are "good for you." What's your opinion?

There is a traditional belief dating back to early German folk potters that salt kiln vapors are good for a cold, and this tale is about as healthful as the English potters' folk tale that excessive alcohol consumption helps relieve lead poisoning. Salt kilns emit hydrochloric acid vapors which, in addition to deteriorating the metal parts of anything nearby, also can damage the potter's lungs. These vapors should be avoided, particularly by those with long-term, occupational exposure. With all the interest in healthful practices lately, it is not hard to find a potter wearing a dust respirator during salt glazing, but such equipment is patently useless for this purpose. Rather, an acid gas canister must be used in such a respirator before it offers sufficient protection during salt glazing. Such canisters are available from the major manufacturers of NIOSH-approved respirators and their dealers. See "Safety Equipment and Clothing" in the Yellow Pages, or consult your local ceramics supplier.

I fire an electric kiln nearly every day in our school art room, and while there is some ventilation through open windows near the kiln, there is a strong smell of sulfur in the air during firing (particularly bisque firings)—sometimes enough to irritate eyes, both mine and the students'. Could you comment on whether or not this is a health hazard?

Good ventilation is imperative in school situations, particularly for the health of the teacher who is likely to have a lifetime exposure to kiln gases and ceramic materials.

In their second edition of the book *Ceramic Science for the Potter*, W.G. Lawrence and R.R. West comment that "gaseous sulfur oxides are very toxic. Both SO_2 and SO_3 can produce lung injury at small concentrations of 5 to 10 ppm (parts per million). Each can combine with water vapor to form acid aerosols which (even) damage vegetation, metals and fabrics. At concentrations of 5 ppm, SO_2 is irritating to the eyes and respiratory system."

It appears that many teachers fear discussing ventilation requirements with their school administrators because of concerns that such requests might jeopardize the ceramics program. Nevertheless, the health of students and teachers in art requires the same attention to ventilation as is typically applied in science. Alternatives for safe kiln ventilation from the most reliable to the least are: electric kilns should be placed outdoors; or in a room away from the classroom (with its own ventilation system); should have an exhaust system if placed in the classroom; or should receive sufficient cross ventilation or "negative pressure" ventilation that kiln gases are directed out-of-doors.

Can you provide some general information on kiln emissions? Have there been any recent tests to actually measure for sulfur, lead, carbon monoxide, etc., in the air around kilns?

In recent tests conducted by Parker C. Reist, Chapel Hill, North Carolina, emissions from bisque and Cone 06 glaze firings in a 3½-cubic-foot and a 7-cubic-foot electric kiln were examined. Located in a small laboratory room (12×18×9 feet) with one door usually left open, the kilns were fired without ventilation, with a fan or with a hood. Air samples were collected at 1 foot above the kiln lid, 7 inches from the kiln; and at 5 feet above the floor, 2 feet from the front of the kiln.

A series of 18 firings (six bisque, six with a commercial glaze containing lead and cadmium, and six with a commercial glaze containing lithium) were monitored. Only the amount of carbon monoxide during the unventilated bisque firing exceeded the threshold limit values (TLV) recommended by the American Conference of Governmental Industrial Hygienists.

The TLV for carbon monoxide is 50 ppm. During the tests, the largest concentration measured was 400 ppm, at the closest sampling area to the small kiln after three and a half hours of firing with no ventilation. (Peak carbon monoxide levels are reached well before peak temperature.) Just by supplying simple dilution ventilation (a fan) the concentration remained below the recommended TLV.

In general, sulfur dioxide results for the greenware firings were quite low—0.1 ppm or less, well under the TLV of 2 ppm. The higher SO_2 levels appeared to be due to the type of clay used. The levels of formaldehyde measured at the different sampling locations also remained well below the TLV of 1 ppm; the highest concentration (at the unventilated kiln) was 0.559 ppm. Again, ventilation greatly improved the readings to the point that no formaldehyde was detected when the hood exhaust was used for greenware firings in either kiln.

Without exception, metal samples (lead, cadmium, barium and lithium) collected from the air around the kilns during the glaze firings showed little if any present. In fact, because the fan or hood had little or no effect on metal contamination percentages, it can be assumed the measurings represent background sources.

Also, carbon monoxide levels were not as important a factor during the glaze firings as compared to the bisque. The highest average concentration for the unventilated kilns was 27.9 ppm.

The conclusion to be drawn from this study is that providing some ventilation (a fan is good, an exhaust system is better) should eliminate concentrations of hazardous elements in kiln room air—particularly carbon monoxide.

Ceramic Raw Materials

Material	Formula	Molecular Weight	Equivalent Weight	Fired Formula
Aluminum Hydroxide	$Al_2(OH)_6$	156	156	Al_2O_3
Barium Carbonate	$BaCO_3$	197	197	BaO
Bone Ash	$Ca_3(PO_4)_2$	310	103	CaO
Borax	$Na_2O \cdot 2B_2O_3 \cdot 10H_2O$	382	382	$Na_2O \cdot 2B_2O_3$
Boric Acid	$B_2O_3 \cdot 3H_2O$	124	124	B_2O_3
Colemanite (Calcium Borate)	$2CaO \cdot 3B_2O_3 \cdot 5H_2O$	412	206	$2CaO \cdot 3B_2O_3$
Cryolite	Na_3AlF_6	210	420	$3Na_2O \cdot Al_2O_3$
Dolomite	$CaCO_3 \cdot MgCO_3$	184	184	$CaO \cdot MgO$
Feldspar, Potash (theoretical)	$K_2O \cdot Al_2O_3 \cdot 6SiO_2$	557	557	same
Feldspar, Soda (theoretical)	$Na_2O \cdot Al_2O_3 \cdot 6SiO_2$	524	524	same
Flint (Silica, Quartz)	SiO_2	60	60	same
Fluorspar	CaF_2	78	78	CaO
Kaolin (China Clay)	$Al_2O_3 \cdot 2SiO_2 \cdot 2H_2O$	258	258	$Al_2O_3 \cdot 2SiO_2$
Lead, Red	Pb_3O_4	684	228	PbO
Lead, White	$2PbCO_3 \cdot Pb(OH)_2$	775	258	PbO
Lead, Yellow (Litharge)	PbO	223	223	same
Lepidolite	$LiF \cdot KF \cdot Al_2O_3 \cdot 3SiO_2$	356	356	same
Lithium Carbonate	Li_2CO_3	74	74	Li_2O
Magnesium Carbonate	$MgCO_3$	84	84	MgO
Pearl Ash	K_2CO_3	138	138	K_2O
Petalite	$Li_2O \cdot Al_2O_3 \cdot 8SiO_2$	197	197	same
Pyrophyllite	$Al_2O_3 \cdot 4SiO_2 \cdot H_2O$	360	360	$Al_2O_3 \cdot 4SiO_2$
Soda Ash	Na_2CO_3	106	106	Na_2O
Sodium Bicarbonate	$NaHCO_3$	84	168	Na_2O
Spodumene	$Li_2O \cdot Al_2O_3 \cdot 4SiO_2$	372	372	same
Strontium Carbonate	$SrCO_3$	148	148	SrO
Talc	$3MgO \cdot 4SiO_2 \cdot H_2O$	379	126	$3MgO \cdot 4SiO_2$
Tin Oxide	SnO_2	151	151	same
Titanium Dioxide	TiO_2	80	80	same
Whiting	$CaCO_3$	100	100	CaO
Wollastonite	$Ca \cdot SiO_3$	116	116	same
Zinc Oxide	ZnO	81	81	same
Zircopax	$ZrO_2 \cdot SiO_2$	183	183	same
Zirconium Oxide	ZrO_2	123	123	same

Colorants

Material	Formula	Molecular Weight	Equivalent Weight	Fired Formula
Chromic Oxide	Cr_2O_3	152	152	same
Cobalt Carbonate	$CoCO_3$	119	119	CoO
Cobalt Oxide, Black	Co_3O_4	241	80	CoO
Copper Carbonate	$CuCO_3$	124	124	CuO
Copper Oxide (Cupric)	CuO	80	80	same
Copper Oxide (Cuprous)	Cu_2O	143	80	CuO
Iron Chromate	$FeCrO_4$	172	172	same
Iron Oxide, Red (Ferric)	Fe_2O_3	160	160	same
Iron Oxide, Black (Ferrous)	FeO	72	72	same
Manganese Carbonate	$MnCO_3$	115	115	MnO
Manganese Dioxide, Black	MnO_2	87	87	same
Nickel Oxide, Green	NiO	75	75	same
Nickel Oxide, Black	Ni_2O_3	166	83	NiO
Rutile (Titanium Dioxide, Impure)	TiO_2	80	80	same

Temperature Equivalents for Orton Standard Pyrometric Cones

Cone Number	Large Cones 150°C*	270°F*	Cone Number	Small Cones 300°C*	540°F*
022	586	1086	022	630	1165
021	614	1137	021	643	1189
020	635	1175	020	666	1231
019	683	1261	019	723	1333
018	717	1323	018	752	1386
017	747	1377	017	784	1443
016	792	1458	016	825	1517
015	804	1479	015	843	1549
014	838	1540	014	870	1596
013	852	1566	013	880	1615
012	884	1623	012	900	1650
011	894	1641	011	915	1680
010	894	1641	010	919	1686
09	923	1693	09	955	1751
08	955	1751	08	983	1801
07	984	1803	07	1008	1846
06	999	1830	06	1023	1873
05	1046	1915	05	1062	1944
04	1060	1940	04	1098	2008
03	1101	2014	03	1131	2068
02	1120	2048	02	1148	2098
01	1137	2079	01	1178	2152
1	1154	2109	1	1179	2154
2	1162	2124	2	1179	2154
3	1168	2134	3	1196	2185
4	1186	2167	4	1209	2208
5	1196	2185	5	1221	2230
6	1222	2232	6	1255	2291
7	1240	2264	7	1264	2307
8	1263	2305	8	1300	2372
9	1280	2336	9	1317	2403
10	1305	2381	10	1330	2426
11	1315	2399	11	1336	2437
12	1326	2419	12	1355	2471

*Degree of temperature rise per hour.

Kiln Atmosphere Colors and Corresponding Temperatures (Approximate)

Color	Cone	°F	°C
Dull Red Glow	022	1080	580
Dark Red	019	1220	660
Cherry Red	014	1530	830
Red-Orange	010	1680	915
Orange	05	1900	1040
Yellow-Orange	1	2120	1160
Yellow	4	2170	1185
Yellow-White	6	2250	1230
White	10	2380	1305
Brilliant White	15	2600	1425
Dazzling White	20	2800	1540

Temperature Conversion

To convert a Centigrade temperature to Fahrenheit multiply the temperature by 9/5 and add 32:
$100°C \times 9/5 = 180 + 32 = 212°F$

To convert Fahrenheit to Centigrade subtract 32 and multiply the answer by 5/9:
$212°F - 32 = 180 \times 5/9 = 100°C$